"David Treadway is known far and wide as a therapist's therapist. He is a consummate clinician whose fingerprints have become an indelible mark on thousands of therapists across North America. *Treating Couples Well* is the summation of his life's work—an inside look at what actually goes on behind closed doors—how a highly gifted healer thinks blow by blow. Brimming with insight and practical tips, Treadway makes a superb guide for any couple therapist new and overwhelmed or experienced and in need of inspiration."

—**Terry Real**, author of *The New Rules of Marriage: What You Need to Know to Make Love Work*

"Bravo! This book is a clinical game-changer! It teaches readers that couple therapy is not simply a matter of teaching relationship skills or following a strict, unvarying protocol with every couple; it's about the artful blend of utilizing theory and more importantly, the healing therapeutic relationship. As Treadway unpacks his therapy approach, readily apparent are his vast expertise from years of being in the trenches with couples along with his own long-term marriage, his warmth, vulnerability and profound respect for clients.

As a therapist specializing in on-the-brink couples for nearly 4 decades, as well as someone who is also in a very long-term marriage, the lessons in this book ring true and are invaluable. Anyone working with couples (or for that matter, in a relationship themselves) will benefit from Treadway's astute perspectives on how to help people love each other more completely."

— ***Michele Weiner-Davis***, author of *Divorce Busting* and *Healing from Infidelity*

"This is the kind of wisdom we hope for from our old masters. Psychotherapists of all ages, but especially the young, will feel informed, held, pushed, and pushed again. Every one of them will emerge from this plunge into the living heart of marital therapy a more confident and competent professional."

—**Barry Dym, PhD**, co-author of *Couples: Exploring and Understanding the Cycles of Intimate Relationships*

"Like a master chef opening his book of favorite recipes, David Treadway invites us to sample and savor a collaborative approach to caring for couples. *Treating Couples Well* is a personal and practical guide for new and seasoned therapists alike. The 'art and the mystery' that comprise the craft of couples therapy are well situated within a collaborative framework for those whose love's been lost, hidden, or awaiting the hope of transformation. Treats are best enjoyed when they are shared—our thanks to David Treadway for sharing his life's wisdom."

—**Jay Lappin, MSW, LCSW**, Minuchin Center for the Family

TREATING COUPLES WELL

Treating Couples Well shows clinicians how to create a collaborative approach to couple therapy, which will empower couples to take charge of their own treatment.

Written in an engaging and conversational style, the book carefully explains how to help couples choose between a variety of clinical approaches and offers effective treatment strategies for a wide range of issues, including infidelity, intimacy and sexuality, communication, mental illness, and addiction. Chapters also explore the importance of considering the therapist's own life experience and its impact on working with couples. Practical interventions, clinical vignettes, and homework exercises are included throughout to help therapists to successfully support the needs of each couple and to encourage meaningful work between sessions.

Drawing on a plethora of case examples from the career of a leading couple therapist, *Treating Couples Well* will be a valuable resource to couple and marriage and family therapists at all levels.

David C. Treadway, PhD, is a nationally known couple therapist and author who has been teaching workshops and conducting training around the USA for the past forty years. He has written four other books and is the award-winning author of over thirty articles. Dr. Treadway has appeared on *Good Morning America*, 20/20 and other television and radio shows, and formerly hosted his own radio program on family communications.

TREATING COUPLES WELL

A Practical Guide to Collaborative Couple Therapy

David C. Treadway

Routledge
Taylor & Francis Group
NEW YORK AND LONDON

First published 2020
by Routledge
52 Vanderbilt Avenue, New York, NY 10017

and by Routledge
2 Park Square, Milton Park, Abingdon, Oxon, OX14 4RN

Routledge is an imprint of the Taylor & Francis Group, an informa business

Library of Congress Cataloging-in-Publication Data
A catalog record for this title has been requested

ISBN: 978-0-415-78774-1 (hbk)
ISBN: 978-0-415-78775-8 (pbk)
ISBN: 978-1-315-22575-3 (ebk)

Typeset in Joanna
by Swales & Willis, Exeter, Devon, UK

CONTENTS

ACKNOWLEDGMENTS

First, my couples. I have had the privilege of working with several thousand couples over the past forty-five years. I have helped many of them, and I have not helped many of them. Success and failure have both been my teachers. Every couple I have ever seen has helped me become the best therapist and even the best person I can be. I want to thank each and every one of them.

My book is built around a myriad of case examples and dialogue. Obviously, I have drawn from my experience working with couples but I have carefully fictionalized all the clinical material to protect the identities of my actual clients.

Over the years, I have developed a lot of how I do couple work on my own, but I have been profoundly influenced by my colleagues and peers. In many instances, I am not sure what are my ideas and what I have absorbed from many others too numerous to name But I want to particularly thank Harville Hendrix and Helen Hunt for their work on active listening, Janis Abrams Springs for her work on healing couples after affairs, Michele Weiner Davis's work on intimacy and the Gottmans for all of their work. Some of my ideas in these areas have been adapted from their work. I particularly want to thank Dan Wile, who coined the term Collaborative Couple Therapy before I did, and yet he has been graciously willing to accept my use of the term for my couple work.

I also want to acknowledge Bill Doherty's discernment work with couples considering divorce. Years ago, I created my own version of working with couples dealing with whether to go or stay and only recently discovered how much my efforts are very similar to his seminal work in this area. I strongly recommend his more complete body of work in *Helping Couples on the Brink of Divorce: Discernment Counseling for Troubled Relationships* (Doherty and Harris).

I also want to acknowledge my use throughout this book of ideas and writings I have done in prior books and articles. This book reflects my life's work, and I have utilized materials that I have written about throughout my career. So I would particularly like to thank my prior publishers of my books: Norton (*Before It's Too Late: Working with Substance Abuse in Families*), Basic (*Dead Reckoning: A Therapist Confronts his Own Grief*), Guilford (*Intimacy, Change and Other Therapeutic Mysteries*), Union Square Press (*Home Before Dark: A Family Portrait of Cancer and Healing*), Routledge (*Psychotherapists Revealed: Therapists Speak about Self-Disclosure in Therapy*).

I also want to express my appreciation for using some of my prior material from the *Psychotherapy Networker*, which has been publishing my articles for more than thirty-five years.

Then there are my writing mentors, without whom this book and everything else I have ever written would have been impossible. First and foremost, there was Rich Simon of the *Psychotherapy Networker*, who literally taught me how to write, beginning with my first article in 1986. And he still teaches me how to write. Cindy Barrilleaux helped me and held my hand on three prior books and numerous articles. Candace Johnson, my personal editor, has done a superb job in helping me write this book line by line with great cheer, and gentle, but firm feedback. Clare Ashworth, my Routledge editor, has taken up the baton and been a steady support for this effort with great enthusiasm and skill. I thank all of you from the bottom of my heart.

My wife sometimes teases me and says, "It takes a village to raise a David," and it's true that I have had a wealth of teachers, mentors, guides, and even therapists through the years. Thanks to Jeff Schlicter, Robert Klein, Jay Haley, Sal Minuchin, Faye Snider, Barbara Greenspan, Nancy Riemer, my best friend, Barry Dym and my brother, Jim.

In recent years, I have been helped on my continuing healing and spiritual journey by Laurie Watt and Narayan Liebenson. I am particularly grateful for Laurie and Narayan for their boundless compassion and wisdom and tolerance for this aging soul who does tend to go around and around in circles from time to time.

Speaking of compassion, wisdom, and tolerance brings me to my dearly beloved Kate. We met at a fraternity party in 1965 and spent the evening sitting on a pool table, our legs swinging side by side. And here we are, fifty-four years later, still side by side. Kate's love has been the backbone of my life. She knows me through and through and loves me anyway.

Dearest Kate, thank you for the gift of you. You've made my life possible. I will love you in all ways, always.

me

INTRODUCTION

Last week, John and Ellen sat frozen in place in my office, each with arms crossed protectively over their hearts; each with downcast eyes; each looking grief stricken. They seemed much older and diminished. I hadn't seen them for twelve years.

John looked up at me and said softly, "Maybe it was a mistake."

"What was a mistake, John?" I asked.

"Us working so hard with you to get back together after I had the affair and we were separated. Maybe we should have given up way back then."

Ellen began to cry. Reaching for the tissues, she said, "I'm afraid John's right. Of course, it's not your fault, but we would never have gotten back together without your help and caring. Maybe it really wasn't meant to be. Look at us now. We're too old to get divorced, and we still make each other miserable all the time."

She began sobbing. John wiped his eyes with a tissue. I felt the sting of my own tears. I love these two but hate their marriage. And I had worked my tail off helping them stay together.

"Maybe it was a mistake, you two," I said sadly, "It is heartbreaking to consider the possibility that you might be right."

We sat in silence and tears for a while, grieving together.

Then I softly said, "But you're here now, and maybe we can talk about how to make this a little more tolerable. Maybe—"

"There you go, Dr. T," said Ellen with a smile. "There's no quit in you."

I smiled back. "You're right, Ellen. All three of us may have made a mistake twenty years ago. But you're here right now, and so am I. Do you want to work at this, even though you know leopards don't change their spots and you guys still really grate on each other sometimes?"

"Oh, Christ, what else are we going to do?" John asked with characteristic annoyance.

And so we began anew.

I am sitting at my desk in the predawn light of spring. I just came in from having coffee on my porch, where I heard the liquid beauty of a wood thrush's song. My heart is full of the love and grief of life.

Finally, I'm beginning this book and I am surprised to be opening it with the long, frustrating, sad story of my work with Ellen and John. But their story captures the heart of the matter: trying to make it as a couple can be damned hard; trying to be a successful couple therapist can be damned hard, too. There are no simple diagnostic codes or treatment plans for couple work. The problems are frequently not well defined, nor are there clear metrics for successful outcome. I have been working with couples for forty-five years and can say with conviction that the practice of couple therapy is truly an art and a mystery.

I have had dramatic successes in my work, like the couple in crisis over the husband's affairs and drinking and on the brink of an ugly divorce. After a year of therapy, they had come such a long way that they were referring to their transformed relationship as their "second marriage." I remember the husband saying to me with relish, "You know what I like best about our second marriage, Doc?"

"What's that, Mike?"

"Well, here we are in a brand-new relationship with each other, and the lawyers didn't get a dime!"

In contrast to Mike and his wife is my diligent, loving work with John and Ellen. I was the glue that held them together. Perhaps it was a profound mistake for me to go so many extra miles to keep them together. Yet, they did raise a family together and have a wide community of friends who love and respect them. They each have been very successful, despite not having a very good relationship with one another. Would it have been better for them to have split up all those years ago? Who can say?

I have worked with couples who have stayed together who, I thought, would have been better off if they had divorced. I've also seen couples split up who I thought would have done well if they had stayed together through the tough times.

Aside from years of experience, much of my judgment is heavily influenced by my own relational experience, gender, and family of origin background. My wife and I just celebrated fifty years together. These days we don't talk as much about good days and bad days as about good decades and bad decades. We married in college—two clueless kids. Our first decade was rough. If we'd been a little more mature and emotionally healthy, we might have divorced back then, but we were incredibly enmeshed. Ironically, that gave us the time to grow into a wonderful marriage.

Sometimes, on the weeks when we're a little disconnected, and not particularly intimate, I find myself reassuring my clients that couples can't always feel close, that sexual desire and frequency waxes and wanes, and that it's normal to oscillate between intimacy and distance. At the end of a week of normalizing this stuff with my couples, I feel much better about my own marriage. Hmmm.

Perhaps the personal relationship histories of couple therapists influence how we look at and judge our clients' relationships more than we fully appreciate. Perhaps we even lean toward promoting our solutions for our own relationships. If we are hanging in there in a difficult marriage, do we encourage our clients to do the same? And conversely, if divorce worked for us, is that what we advise? We all bring our own stories to our understanding of couple relationships. And we all have the same question for ourselves as well as our clients: what are the criteria for a "good enough" relationship?

I have come to believe that the essence of my job is not to save marriages, but to help each member of a couple find their "chosen" life, whether it's to accept the complexities and compromises of staying in their relationships or face the challenges and consequences of divorce. Few of us get the happily-ever-after story, but we can learn to take responsibility for our own lives, face the consequences of our actions, and chose our own paths. The poet, Mary Oliver, ends "The Summer Day" with this challenge: "Tell me, what is it you plan to do with your one wild and precious life?" My job is to help the folks I see answer that question.

I'm not likely to help Ellen and John change their battle-hardened relationship. But perhaps I can help them bring some compassion and kindness to the task of accepting each other a little more just as they are, and maybe even forgiving each other for how difficult their journey has been.

***

Most couples come to our offices with an accumulation of hurts from the past, ineffective and hurtful communication in the present, and fear about the future. One or both members of the couple are often haunted by uncertainty about whether their marriage is good enough. Should they stay or should they go?

Couple therapy can easily become bogged down in the morass of too many issues and too little time. It is very difficult for couples to make and sustain progress in some areas of their relationship while learning how to keep unresolved issues from spilling over. In addition, whatever progress they make in a session is often undermined by their returning to old patterns of interaction by the time they are on the way home.

That's why, right from the first session, I try to create a collaborative and empowering therapy that enables couples to discern their own path forward. I help them choose their treatment plan, picking (from three quite different approaches) the one that suits them best. I help them work on defined, discrete issues while they compartmentalize others. I help them work on positive steps while acknowledging and learning to tolerate their resistance, distrust, and vulnerability.

I have found that it's often what happens *between* sessions that determines whether couples will be able to make substantive, sustainable changes. So I do my best to motivate them to work as hard between sessions as during sessions. The couples in my practice that have the most success are those who grow and change through the processes of doing homework and therapeutic exercises at home.

There is certainly no "one size fits all" model for treating couples. However, after forty-five years of doing couple therapy, I have specific treatment approaches for a variety of different couple situations and problems. But all treatment models are simply reference points that allow us generally to know where we are and where we are headed. The actual treatment results from integrating what we see in the couple and the model we are using. The model helps us organize the data, pick out what is significant, anticipate responses, and know which steps might be appropriate next. It is an organizational tool, a way of helping us think about our clients, ourselves, and the course of treatment. But as Gregory Bateson famously said, "The map is not the territory."

In the end, I believe the essence of treating couples well is helping them become more comfortable with each other's discomforts and differences, with sharing their feelings without shame or "shoulds," and with hearing the other's feelings without taking them too personally. Each member of the couple needs to learn how to carefully be true to themselves while in the presence of the other; to apologize and forgive, and to accept their own and their partner's limits and failings with empathy and compassion. In other words, couples need to learn how to live the Serenity Prayer: accepting the things they cannot change, having the courage to change the things they can, and having the wisdom to know the difference.

After all the theories are spoken, all the models considered, and all the techniques applied, the best we have to offer our clients is creating a nurturing sanctuary where they can share their yearnings, fears, and flawed humanity without shame and with deep compassion; where they can dare being vulnerable and take the risk to change.

Couple therapists are not all-knowing guides marching fearlessly ahead of our clients along harrowing mountain trails. Yes, we do have pitons, ropes, and hammers. Yes, many of us have made the climb before. We have maps and weather reports. It is good to have this experience and equipment. But ultimately, our willingness to share the risk, to give gentle voice to the fear, and to hold the sweaty palms is the gift that heals.

It's taken me a lifetime of successes and mistakes to learn how to help couples most of the time, get from here to there by the simplest and best possible route. And yet, sometimes, I still get lost along the way.

This book is just my story of my work with couples. It includes whatever wisdom I have accrued from years of essentially trial and error. Our field is evolving. Folks like the Gottmans, Sue Johnson, Harville Hendrix and Helen Hunt, Esther Perel, Janis Abrams Spring, Bill Doherty, Terry Real, Dick Schwartz, and so many others have articulated great treatment models and techniques, from which I liberally borrow. But this book isn't a summary of the development of couple therapy. It's just my experiences and learnings that I hope will be helpful to you.

I would like *Treating Couples Well* to be a useful guide, even a kind of GPS, for therapists. But most important, I want it to be a supportive companion for all those couples therapists finding their own path after me. This is my life's work. I look forward to sharing it with you.

1

NORMAL CHALLENGES OF LONG-TERM RELATIONSHIPS

Robert looked like he was being drilled at the dentist office as Joan began our session with what was becoming a familiar litany of complaint.

"We spend all our time battling about whose turn it is to take time off from work to go to the kids' parent-teacher conference, and who is doing the shopping. There's never any time for an intimate, friendly conversation. And by the way, having a partner [she threw a darting look at Robert] forget to pick up his child after school is not exactly an aphrodisiac."

"Hold on for a second, Joan," I interrupted. "Unfortunately, you're describing the modern American marriage, which turns out to be an endless round of business negotiations about who is doing what, when, where, and how. It's kind of like the modern couple is now a small business with two CEOs. Not exactly a model that would pass muster at the Harvard Business School. And I'm sure that it's frustrating for you, too, Robert."

Robert looked at me and gave shrug of resignation. "Well, we don't have very many Hallmark moments."

"That's part of our job here," I said. "We need to find ways of separating out the grinding business of being a couple from the intimate, nurturing love making—and I'm not just talking about sex—of being a couple."

And, for a moment, their heads nodded. Together.

Being a successful couple entails some really hard work. I help couples appreciate and accept the difficulties of being a long-term couple in this era when there is so much less institutional, community, religious, and familial support for the sanctity and institution of marriage. The challenges of being in a successful, committed relationship are more daunting than they've ever been.

This is a huge topic, and I will try to give you a kind CliffsNotes summary of some of the particular challenges that couples face in our post-modern society and some of the key qualities and healthy habits couples can develop that can increase their chances of creating stable relational well-being.

First, we are more individually isolated than ever before, often living far from family and friends, which leads to enormous increase of romantic/relational expectations of ourselves and our partners to meet a broad range our emotional needs. We're not just supposed to be lovers, but also partners, best friends, and co-managers of our lives. Throughout most of human history, marital relationships were primarily an economic arrangement with very low expectations of either intense romantic attachment or intimacy. Now the expectation that somehow marriage should meet almost all of our emotional needs has crept into the culture.

Second, until approximately seventy years ago, gender defined the rules of engagement for almost all long-term relationships. Roles and power distributions were thoroughly defined as were methods for decision making and problem solving. Men and women spent the vast majority of their lives in the company of their same sex and not each other. Even sexuality was, for the most part, a protection racket: male sexual entitlement in exchange for physical and economic security.

Third, marriages usually were made within one's own tribe or cultural group. Interpersonal styles, communication patterns, and normative behaviors were familiar to each partner and conformed to their expectations. Nowadays, individuals have much more ethnic, religious, and racial freedom in their marital choices. Each member might come from a sharply different culture with very idiosyncratic notions about what marriage *should* be like. Rarely are these expectations fully conscious much less negotiated by the couple as they set off into a shared life.

Fourth, in the past forty years, there has been a rapid increase of acknowledged and accepted diversity of sexual orientations and fluidity of gender identity. The increasingly broad acceptance of gay marriage, transgendered people, and gender questioning folks has transformed the definition of a "normal" marriage. Despite the ongoing, strong backlash, traditionally accepted norms of relational and sexual behavior are being expanded and redefined as the culture becomes more inclusive and accepting of diversity.

With all these changes in our post-feminist, multicultural, pluralistic era, virtually every aspect of being a couple (gay or straight) is a nonstop round of negotiation and frequently conflict. Couples have to negotiate and balance their careers, parenting, household chores, social and familial relationships, as well as intimacy and sexuality, all the while expecting each other to be their best friend. Having to create their own hierarchy, rules of engagement, role definitions, and, essentially, their own culture is a relentlessly draining activity. At the same time, societal expectations that each person be the source of nourishing almost all intimate and sexual needs creates a perfect storm for conflict and disappointment.

Given the modern high pressures of a committed relationship, the divorce rate of nearly 50 percent and the huge increase of people who have already survived their parents' divorce, the question "Is our marriage good enough" often underlies the tensions and struggles couples go through. Couples come for treatment for a wide variety of idiosyncratic presenting problems, but the underlying question of whether their marriage is viable is often the core issue that hangs over many couples like the proverbial Sword of Damocles

Common Obstacles Most Couples Face

Being a successful couple (again, gay or straight) is often like learning how to ride in a steeplechase. These are some of the difficult jumps to be mastered around the course.

Transitioning from Being "In Love" to Being "In Life"

Neuroscience has now revealed that the "in love" experience that has been idealized since the beginning of time in song, poetry, art, and music is similar to the heightened state of joy and euphoria created by drugs like cocaine and Ecstasy. The same parts of the brain are activated. Helen Fisher and other neuroscientists have shown that the heightened state of well-being created by hormonal flooding leads to the falling-in-love experience. This brain state is neither discriminating nor relationally attuned and has a natural shelf life of about eighteen months. However, it's this short-lived but extremely powerful romantic attachment that draws people into lifelong commitments. Although this serves the need to perpetuate the species, it can be misleading for picking a life partner. I refer to it with my clients as "nature's bait and switch."

New couples may begin by opening their hearts and sharing whatever is on their minds, and they may feel known and loved more than ever before; they even feel unconditional love flowing between them. Then, suddenly, they discover that their partner has all the usual flaws and failings of normal humans. The honeymoon is over, and they are transitioning into a shared life. This is often when they first truly wound each other and begin to develop unsuccessful, dysfunctional ways of responding to those wounds.

New couples may begin to try learn how to give each other gentle critical feedback, like Charlie saying sweetly to James, "Honey, could you take a little bit more time with warming things up before going for the main event. I need to feel more connected before we do it." And James replies with, "I thought you liked how assertive I can be." Now they're off to the races. Feeling misunderstood, Charles says, "I wasn't being critical about your sexual techniques, I was just trying to share my own needs." And James suddenly feels inadequate. Things can deteriorate quickly into who is feeling more criticized and/or who is overly sensitive.

Couples handle these tensions with all kinds of responses. It might become a debate, or they might lapse into silence; one member of the couple might take the blame and harbor resentment; they might try to "kiss and make up" while one or both of them are still stewing. These ways of handling hurt feelings that get started early in the life of the couple often become rigid patterns of interaction that get repeated for years before the couple ever comes into the office.

Although many couples "fall in love" before entering marriage and life commitments, others choose a life together without the romantic fireworks of the "in love" experience. They may get together because it's the right time to settle down or because they've been too hurt by a prior relationship or they have an unplanned pregnancy. Even without the foundation of an intense romantic passion, they, too, go through a let-down effect as they transition from a good-enough intimate friendship into a committed life. One or both members often feel the pain of not having had the spark from the beginning. That too can lead to difficult patterns of interaction that mask an underlying disengagement and disappointment.

In addition to all the common issues of two individuals learning how to share a life and partner with each other, couples bring their childhood, hurts, disappointments, and yearnings, as well as expectations about what family life is like. Often, the intense challenges of growing up in a particular family—like being emotionally or sexually abused, or being a gay child in a culturally conservative family, or being a child of divorce or addiction—leave profound wounds. Most couples, as they create their own new, intimate relationships and families, hope to resolve and heal from their family-of-origin wounds.

In this first phase of a shared life, regardless of how the relationship began, it's often impossible for couples to directly share their frustrations, let-downs, disappointments, and doubts with each other without hurting each other's feelings. Each member of the couple tends to handle these feelings on their own, which can separate them at the deepest emotional level. Regardless of the presenting problem they bring to our offices, these underlying issues, developed in the beginning of the committed relationship, are still at the heart of the couple's pain.

Almost all couples have a shadow of hurt, disappointment—even anger—within despite how successful they appear outwardly. I frequently make this point at workshops by playfully saying, "I may not be able to help every couple, but give me one hour with any couple, no matter how happy they say they are, and I can wreck their relationship." Yes, more than a little provocative hyperbole there, but what I mean is that with focused questioning, I could expose the heartaches, hurts, difficult compromises, disappointments, and yearnings that one or both members of a couple have tucked away somewhere in their hearts. The quote "Men lead lives of quiet desperation" applies all too commonly to couples, too.

When Two Become Three

Becoming parents is both extraordinarily bonding for couples and potentially divisive. Obviously, the couple relationship loses a degree of primacy as the parents integrate an infant into their lives. Again, as when couples start down their path together, becoming pregnant and having a baby is idealized as a time of peak marital bliss. Yet the baby will come first from there on out, and couples' adjustment to the change in their priorities is often difficult. Not only is their intimate life likely to be disrupted, but most of their nurturing, affectionate, loving behavior will be redirected to the infant instead of each other. Add in sleep deprivation, oftentimes two jobs, and the challenges of child care, and the couple relationship is pushed not only to the back burner, but usually off the stove entirely.

Couples usually make these adjustments without negotiation or complaint as they strive to become the best parents they can be. The precious, tender nature of welcoming a child into the world and the expectation that this is a wildly joyful event can inhibit sharing their doubts and disappointments about their experience of parenting with each other. So they each manage their difficult feelings alone. Difficult patterns of interaction often mask the underlying, unspoken tensions caused by all the changes couples must make. For example, "I think you are overanxious about the baby. All you do is worry about every little thing" can be code for "You are not paying any attention to me," or "Why don't *you* change her in the middle of the night and feed her a bottle, so I can get a good night's sleep for once?" can also mean "I don't feel like you're there for me."

The Long Leaving-Home Journey

After the onslaught of children, the next developmental stage for couples is the inevitable tension in the family around parenting adolescents and young adults. Today, the time of childhood innocence and purity has shrunk dramatically as early onset puberty, social media and TV culture, as well as peer pressures have accelerated kids' development and their demands for autonomy and freedom. As described in the previous paragraph, parents adapt their couple relationship to the demands of early parenting. Then, when they face the new challenges of children's demands for independence, as well as the underlying anticipation of the empty-nest syndrome, couples often hit a relational crisis. Parenting, particularly with oppositional kids experimenting with reckless behaviors, becomes much tougher if the couple doesn't agree on how to find the best compromises and the right balance between being "tough" and being "loving."

Any tensions about their own connection and intimacy issues that have been long deferred may underlie their battles about how best to manage the kids. A fight between a couple of parents that began as an argument simply about their teenager's curfew might morph into a huge conflict about their lack of sexual intimacy, or alcohol abuse, or a suspicion of an affair.

This stage of a couple's life also collides with the midlife crisis of the individuals in a way that further drives them into potential conflict, transgressions, and even doubts about the marriage going forward. Folks in their late forties and early fifties often privately wonder about the viability and quality of their relationship as they consider thirty-plus more years together without the unifying bond of keeping the family together. Given that divorce is a socially accepted alternative, couples often ask the question, "Is this marriage good enough?" In addition to crises triggered by affairs and substance abuse, this question is often at the core of what drives couple into therapy. And the harm of living in doubt about whether they should stay together, almost daily evaluating each other's strengths and weaknesses is really corrosive and undermining to the couples' relationship, somewhat akin to the impact of drinking battery acid.

Retirement and Aging

Another common crisis point in relationships comes in response to all the changes and renegotiations couples need to work through as they face retirement issues and inevitable aging and health challenges. A couple's core structure and individual identity has been commonly organized around children and careers for decades. Letting go of both defining roles can rock couples profoundly as they adjust to changes in each other. I remember a wife saying to her newly retired husband, who had been a CEO of a Fortune 500 company, "Listen, George, if you tell me one more time how to load the dishwasher, after I've been doing the dishes for forty years, I'm walking out the door, and you can load them to your heart's content!" A difficult power struggle ensued.

Virtually all aspects of the couple's relationship, roles, expectations, shared vs. individual activities have to be renegotiated at this stage of their lives.

Each of these developmental stages is challenging and often the underlying cause that impels couples toward dysfunctional individual behavior and patterns of relating. By the time couples come for help, they may have made many, many attempts to repair and improve their relationship on their own. Usually one or both of them are in a crisis about whether the relationship can be sustained. That is why, in our first interviews, I usually try to reassure the couple by acknowledging the risks while pointing out the possibilities. "You know," I say, "in Chinese the word 'crisis' is made up of two characters: Danger and Opportunity."

Keys to Success in Long-Term Relationships

Each couple has to find their own path to a workable relationship or even a workable divorce. However, over the years I have found some positive attributes of relating that help couples work out relationships that thrive rather than just survive. None of us is trained on how to be a couple. Part of my job as a therapist is to teach couples ways of relating that can lead them to being happy and fulfilled.

Right from the beginning of a case, I teach couples some of the fundamental behaviors and attitudes useful for creating a strong foundation for a successful relationship. It is not enough to understand and fix problematic issues; often the heart of good therapy is to help clients change aspects of their couple culture–their patterns of interaction that might be habitually harmful and self-defeating. It is essential to help couples create positive patterns, effective and nurturing interactions that build their couple self-esteem; sense of pleasure, appreciation, and competence in their relationship.

I usually integrate the following keys to success into all of my work with couples, regardless of the presenting problem.

1) Couples need to develop balanced, reasonable, and shared expectations about their relationship. Each member comes to the couple with their own family-of-origin, gender perspective, and relational experience, and each usually has individual notions about what a long-term relationship should be like.

With most of the couples, many conflicts are fueled by these fundamentally different expectations. Frequently couples need to accept that their relational expectations need to be made explicit, negotiated, and feel fair. Couples also have to accept that being in a long-term relationship demands a considerable degree of hard work. One expectation that virtually everyone in a marriage begins with is that we should be able express ourselves freely with our partners. Not true. Unconditional love ends by the time we are two (except during the delusion of the "in love" stage). Just expressing your feelings and opinions without considering how they may affect your partner can do harm. A high percentage of couples treat each other and speak to each other in harsh and critical ways that they would never use when speaking to a friend, colleague, or even a stranger.

We have to learn how to be *careful* (full of care) for each other. None of us humans is lovable all the time. We need to work hard to bring our better selves to our relationships, while also tolerating and not being over-reactive to our partners' limitations.

2) Couples need to learn the art of staying close in spite of difficult and unresolved conflicts. Conflict is an unrelenting reality for most couples, and most of us respond to interpersonal conflict with the fight/flight/freeze responses. Couples either turn on each other more (fight), or turn away from each other (flight), or shut down emotionally (freeze). These lead couples down the rabbit hole of dysfunctional relationship patterns like the "distancer-pursuer" dance, the "blowup-and-make-up" routine, or "the ships passing in the night" option.

I teach couples to counter to turn toward each other. Having constructive conflict in safe ways with agreed-upon rules of engagement allows couples to manage conflict as a team, and, even more importantly, helps them maintain intimacy and closeness. They need to learn how to separate the business of relationship from its intimacy. Couples must learn how to have their struggles around the management of their lives while maintaining their intimate connection as friends and lovers.

3) No matter how hard we try, we frequently hurt each other's feelings. Couples have to learn to make amends and practice forgiveness. "I am sorry" and "Apology accepted" are just as important in a couple's communication repertoire as "I love you." This is true for the hurts inflicted in everyday life as well as the major transgressions of affairs, abuse, and addictions.

Unfortunately, our good intentions do not necessarily keep us from hurting our partners. When one member of a couple gets their feelings hurt, often the partner responds defensively, trying to justify their behavior or demonstrate that they had good intentions. Too frequently, members of a couple get lost in the debate about who had been thoughtlessly hurtful and who was being "too sensitive" and taking "helpful suggestions" as criticisms. Oddly enough, both members are right. Couples need to learn how to give each other feedback skillfully, and couples need to learn how to take feedback less personally.

Sometimes, couples go overboard in their effort not to hurt their partner's feelings by stuffing their own. For example, Cheryl confided in me that she really didn't like sex with Tom, but felt that being a loving partner meant not hurting his feelings by talking about it. The result of this caring choice led to her being unfulfilled in her own sexual needs; servicing Tom was a chore, like doing the laundry, and that generated resentment and distance. This had a domino effect on them both. Tom felt that Cheryl wasn't really "into" him, which made him feel insecure and undesirable, which in turn made him feel initiating sex was a burden for her, which led him to stop asking for sex to avoid pressuring her, which made her feel guiltier and like a failure as a wife. By the time they came into see me, they were both sad and hurt and had no sexual life at all. Yet each of them had done their best to be sensitive and caring of the other.

So in addition to being careful about being too blunt, open, and critical of our partners, couples also need to learn the skills to bring up and discuss with their partner their hurt, frustration, or disappointment, and their partner needs to learn to listen with empathy and compassion. The core challenge of almost all couples work is to learn how to safely and gently talk about the underlying pain, vulnerability, and yearning they both carry inside.

4) It's essential that couples learn how to partner well in the business of life, while also finding ways to sustain and nurture the romantic, intimate side of being a couple. Most of us want some version of a Hallmark relationship, with unconditional love and acceptance, in which partners are naturally loving, spontaneously affectionate, and turned on by each other. Unfortunately, long-term relationships entail constant rounds of logistical and management discussions. Intimacy and romance tend to fade into the background. I teach couples to have regular, formal business meetings on the one hand and scheduled time for closeness/intimacy and even sex on the other.

When it comes to intimacy and sex, too often couples are dependent on being in the right "mood," having the same level of yearning and desire, or having a large chunk of time alone to reconnect romantically. That can lead to erratic and hurtful interactions around sexual and romantic overtures. Couples need to learn the value of scheduled, planned times in the rhythm of the week when they put aside the work of the relationship and make time for each other's relational and sexual needs. I call this "effortful love." It involves unromantic logistical planning to make time for romance, regardless of whether they are in the mood. Effortful love also includes planning some routine weekly nurturing behavior, where members of the couple take turns putting the other's needs first. Teaching couples how to care for each other even when they don't feel like it and helping couples learn how to alternate whose needs get met are fundamentally important aspects of helping couples sustain their relationship.

5) It is essential that couples focus on appreciating the positive aspects of each other and their relationship more than on the negative. This is extremely hard for most of us human beings who, by nature,

focus on what's wrong with our partner and what we wish they would do differently, as opposed to feeling gratitude for what our partner does do and appreciation for who he or she is. And we frequently take our partner for granted. I remember one husband of thirty-two years whose wife implored him to tell he loved her every once in a while. He responded by saying with some exasperation, "Well, I married you, didn't I?"

6) Couples need to learn to see each of their limitations, failings, and vulnerabilities with tenderness and compassion. In trying to hold each member of the couple in my therapy room with empathy and kindness, I am hoping to model a way of seeing and experiencing each other. Almost all of us have been hurt and wounded in our childhoods and our prior couple relationships. We bring our insecurities and guardedness into our marriages. Couples need to step back and see their suffering partner with empathy and compassion even though their partner's behavior is frequently wounding to them. For example, early in my own marriage, my wife's experience of having been hurt in a prior relationship and my emotionally shutting down in the wake of my mother's suicide contributed to our difficulty with intimacy. Out of our woundedness, we wounded each other. It took us years of hard work to learn to hold each other's pain with love and compassion, even though we had been hurtful to each other.

***

There are many commonalities in issues and developmental stages that couples go through, and there are some common elements that help create successful relationships. However, there is no one-size-fits-all model for being a couple or for treating a couple. The challenge for couple therapists is to discover and support what will work for each couple.

We are like custom tailors: we have to discover the customer's needs and tastes, take careful measurements, help them make style and fabric choices, and then tailor the finished outfit to fit them well.

2

CREATING COLLABORATIVE COUPLE THERAPY

First Interview

Jane and Sarah were at each other with words and tears. The blame game had started the minute they came into the room.

"You know, I had to drag her here. Sarah doesn't really care anymore about making this work," Jane said almost before they both sat down.

Sarah burst into tears and looked at me imploringly. "See, everything is always my fault."

As I usually do with new clients, I made attempts to join with them. It took a while. I said, "I can tell you have a lot of built-up feelings coming into this meeting, but allow me to play a little catch-up and get to know the two of you before we get back into what brought you here."

Some of my normal opening questions include: How long have you been together? Are you married? Do you have children? What do you do best together? In what way is your relationship better or worse than your parents? How have these issues impacted your intimate life?

After drawing out Sarah and Jane, I added, "By the way, as an aging heterosexual male, if I make any dumb, stereotypical assumptions about you two young women, please don't be polite. Speak up. All couples are a culture unto themselves, and I hope to learn about yours."

I then gave them each a little time to describe their versions of the presenting problem.

However, rather than going to work on the presenting problem, I offered them what I call my Menu of Possibilities: several quite different ways of focusing the couples work.

"We could work on making positive changes in the here and now, or focus on healing the accumulated wounds of your past, or visit the dynamics of your family of origin and see how that has shaped your relationship. Why don't you talk with each other about what path might be best for you."

I paused.

Their silence ensued. A tilt of a head. A slight "hmmm." A faraway gaze. They had never thought of a question like this before. They had no prepared answer available. They were suddenly just in the here and now in my office.

I could hear the grandfather clock ticking. I waited.

It was a good silence.

Couples often come into therapy at war with each other, and like lawyers or siblings, they usually have prepared briefs to present in front of the judge or the parent. Each of them wants to "win" the argument; each of them wants the therapist to be on their side. Thus, they are surprised and unprepared when they are invited to be in a collaborative conversation directly with each other: asked to work together to come up with what treatment approach might be best for both of them.

This unexpected opportunity for them to select treatment priorities is an effective way of empowering couples, while also creating a positive and safe therapeutic culture. I encourage them to take charge of their treatment, enter into a conversation that they've never had before, and practice being a collaborative team. I help them weigh the pros and cons, and usually by the end of the first session they've chosen their own approach to their therapy. This process of their choosing what to work on and what to defer gives them a sense of ownership of their therapy as well as an initial success in making decisions together. It also provides an opportunity for me to coach them into trying more positive pathways of communicating to help them learn how to listen well to each other without interrupting and attacking each other. From the beginning of our work together, I am helping them practice becoming an effective collaborative partnership in improving their relationship.

The session with Sarah and Jane continued.

"So, could you say more about what each of these choices really looks like? I am a little confused," said Jane, breaking the silence. Sarah nodded her head in agreement.

"Sure, bear with me," I said. "This will sound a little like I am being a talk show host. So, behind door number one is what I call *Today is the first day of the rest of your life*, and it really means starting fresh with new skills and approaches to being a couple in spite of the accumulated difficulties, hurts, anger, failure you might have had in the past. We will focus on helping you learn new ways to communicate, manage conflict, negotiate decisions effectively, nurture each other, and even enhance your intimacy and sexuality. It's a lot like taking an intensive course in being a couple with the emphasis on building skills, learning new approaches to old problems, changing how you do things at home. If you choose this method, I'll be giving you a lot of specific techniques and a lot of homework to learn how to do on your own.

"Behind door number two is just the opposite. It's called the *Amends and Forgiveness Protocol*. We begin by calling a truce in the relationship. Instead of trying to work on making things better, we help you co-exist while putting the emphasis of our work on really hearing how much each of you has been hurt in this relationship, making amends to each other for the harm you've done, and learning how to let go and forgive. We wouldn't be just refighting old fights. It's a very structured process that is focused on a safe and compassionate way of helping you heal the wounds that have hurt over the whole history of the relationship. By the time a couple is in my office, they have hurt each other and tried to start over endlessly. Many couples need to find a way of dealing with the enormous hurt, anger, sadness, and disappointments that have already occurred in the relationship before they can really work on changing it.

"I call door number three, the family of origin which involves actually going farther back and starting with the impact on each of you of the family culture you grew up in. Almost all of us have our expectations and yearnings about what we say we want in our adult relationship, which is shaped to a degree by the issues and challenges of growing up in our particular families. Going back and really understanding better how your childhood experience impacted what you brought into this relationship often leads to a much greater understanding and acceptance of the differences that may have divided you right from the beginning. Each of us bring our childhood wounds to our relationship, often with the yearning that our adult love can heal our childhood hurt. And, in addition, given our homophobic culture, often people's experience of 'coming out' to themselves, their families, and to their world has been scarring, and that scarring also shows up in adult relationships.

"Whoops, sorry you two, there I go sounding off like I'm an expert about your experience."

"Don't worry about it, Dr. Treadway. We know you're trying," Sarah said with a kind smile.

"Thanks." I smiled back while noticing that Jane was not smiling.

"Anyway," I went on, "I don't want to overload you with info. The key here is that most couple therapy often flounders around in trying to deal with all three of these issues at once: trying to make changes, dealing with distrust and hurt from the past, and the impact of family dynamics from childhood on the couple's relationship. The heart of this idea is to focus on one thing at a time while putting the rest of the issues on a shelf."

"Don't we have to deal with all this stuff at some point?" Jane pushed back, her tone full of skepticism.

"You're absolutely right, Jane," I responded, appreciating the chance to affirm her. "Many couples choose to do all three of these plans, and we're just choosing the order in which we'll start. However, some couples, having successfully done one step, end up just not feeling the need to open the other doors.

"Now, I have said a lot. Let me be quiet here, and you two talk to each other about which approach appeals most to you. There is no wrong or right answer. My experience is that whatever a couple ends up choosing will be the right answer for them."

More silence.

"Well, I know what you will want," Jane said sharply to Sarah.

Sarah stiffened.

"You probably would guess right, Jane," I interjected, "but why don't you start with what you would like."

Right from the beginning of the conversation, I wanted to help them not fall back on their old conflict style in which Jane was blaming and Sarah was helplessly defending. So I gently redirected.

Jane paused, looks slightly annoyed with me, and then started over.

"Well, I definitely think we should start with changing things now. I really am sick and tired of the way things are, and I would want to see some action, not just talk."

Sarah was on the verge of tears.

I chimed in again. I was trying to set a positive tone to this conversation while acknowledging tough feelings.

"It's okay, Sarah, that Jane has a little edge in her voice. It's clear that she's feeling very hurt and I suspect rejected for a long time. You do get to say what you would choose, but it's really okay for her to have a little hurt, maybe even anger, as we get started on this." I said this to Sarah, but I was really indirectly talking to Jane, and I was pleased to see Jane slightly relax in her seat and her face shift a little from mad to sad.

Jane then said with real sadness and vulnerability, "I just don't feel like you love me anymore."

"That's not true," Sarah responded. "I always feel like you're mad at me all the time."

"It may not feel true to you, Sarah, but Jane is expressing a lot of vulnerability. I suspect you often don't necessarily feel loved by her either."

"That's true," Sarah said with a heavy sigh.

The conversation went on. Sarah proposed the family of origin exploration, which Jane had guessed rightly she would. It became clear that Sarah bore the heavy burden of having been shamed, blamed, and rejected by her conservative family for her sexual orientation and that it had led to ambivalence and insecurity that impacted her comfort and ease with her sexuality in the relationship with Jane. It also became clear that Jane lacked empathy for Sarah and tended to see this all as Sarah's excuse for avoiding intimacy. All of a sudden, we had stumbled into their core wound between them.

Often in first interviews couples get into deeper and more vulnerable material than they know how to handle. I am always aware of the risks of "the car ride home," when they tear into each other about what was said in the session and potentially never come back. I often say to students that "the only real goal of a first session is to make sure there's a second session."

So rather than let Jane and Sarah get lost in their core wound and "blame game," I did intervene with an effort to hold and validate each of them.

"So it seems like this discussion is hard for each of you. I get the sense that for you, Jane, Sarah's wish to discuss her issues with your family of origins feels a little like avoidance of really focusing on improving the relationship, and—"

"You got that right, Doc," Jane interjected.

"But for you, Sarah, it seems like you still carry the weight all the time of your family's angry rejection of who you are, and it may even make it hard to be responsive to some of Jane's hurt and anger."

Sarah nodded and reached for the tissues.

"It may be the case that you guys would benefit from seeing some positive changes in the relationship in order to feel better about each other before you focus on the very painful trauma that is still affecting you today, Sarah. I think you, Jane, might have a lot more empathy and compassion for Sarah around this stuff if the two of you were feeling like you were making demonstrable progress."

They both nodded.

Phew, I thought. "Why don't you discuss a little more how you might feel focusing on learning new skills first."

I knew I was tilting in favor of Jane. I had to make an alliance with her even if it meant not being equally aligned to Sarah in that moment because I felt Jane was actually likely to determine whether they would even come back. Couple therapy isn't 50–50 equal all the time, even though by the end it is very important that both feel equally heard and cared about with compassion.

Jane and Sarah did finally choose to work on improving their communication, decision-making, and nurturing skills: door number 1. And I did my best to prepare them for how to manage trying to change their relational behavior while still having difficult feelings, resentment, and even distrust.

I also invited them to think about what frequency and length of sessions might work best for them. Therapists frequently try to fit clients not only into their model of working but also into their routine time slots. I give clients the chance to choose how often and how long sessions should be. For some clients it works much better to meet with less frequency but over much longer periods of time. I also offer an intensive weekend retreat as well as short sessions over the phone in between office meetings. There is no one-size-fits-all model of therapy, nor is there a right frequency and length of meeting time for folks either.

Jane and Sarah chose to meet in two weeks, and they thought they might want to meet with less frequency and try the phone sessions in between meetings once we got going. They left the office a little less tense and distant. Jane's parting shot as she was headed for the door was, "Well, it wasn't as bad as it could have been," and Sarah looked a little relieved.

It was a start.

3

EFFORTFUL LOVE

Behavioral Change in the Here and Now

"All I ever wanted was for him to bring me flowers. Really, Mother's Day, birthdays, Valentine's Day, Christmas—you name it. For thirty years, he's never done it," Susan repeated throughout our first session.

So at the end of the session, I somewhat flippantly said to John, "So guy, why don't you get her some flowers before our next session?"

And he did.

And she responded by throwing them at him. "Here, take them to your shrink you like so much! All he had to do was ask you once!"

When couples choose the "Today is the first day of the rest of your life" behavioral change option for treatment, they then get to decide whether to work on communication/negotiation/conflict management skills or on nurturing and sexual intimacy. This is my own multifaceted idiosyncratic version of a cognitive behavioral approach to couple therapy, which I will address in the next four chapters before we get to the other possibilities.

When working on learning new skills in relating to each other, it is essential to help couples change behavior while understanding that behavioral change won't necessarily result in their feeling better, closer, safer right away. Just like Susan who threw the flowers, most couples have difficulty trusting and embracing behavioral change even when they are able to make themselves do it.

I often tell the "flowers" story to help couples understand that changing how they communicate and behave with one another when they have accumulated years of disappointments, distrust, and frustration can be very difficult. It's also very challenging to do behavioral change when one isn't feeling positive or close to one's partner. Couples have to learn how to make the disciplined efforts regardless of whether they are in the "mood." And couples have to learn how to accept loving behavior even if it's performed as a dutiful homework exercise rather than something they really want to do. I encourage couples to appreciate the effort the partner is making rather than doubting the purity of their motivation.

This is part of the "effortful love" I described in the last chapter. Despite couples' yearnings for flowing, organic, spontaneous love, the hard work of effortful love is often the marital glue that holds folks together. Sometimes a spouse will push back and say, "But it's not enough that he helps with Christmas shopping, I want him to want to help."

And I will say, "We actually need to bring our professional work selves to the project of being a successful couple." For example, I often respond, at least to my 8:00 am couples, with a playful smile, "So do you really think I wanted to see you this early in the morning? I actually would prefer to be upstairs in bed with a cup of coffee and the *New York Times*." I always get a startled response, and then they get the point.

The challenge is to help couples change at home rather than talk about change in my office. Couples are dominated by their habits and patterns. Frequently, couples may discover and express deep insights or profound, cathartic emotions in our sessions, but by the time they are on the car ride home, they have retreated to habitual ways of relating to each other and their lives. Often the afterglow of a wonderful breakthrough session doesn't last the drive.

Helping couples do "homework" is the heart of building effortful love. As most couple therapists will tell you, it's very difficult to get couples to do it. Before I tell you what homework assignments work particularly well for me, let me first go over the whole challenge of getting couples to do homework.

Motivating Couples to Do Homework

As they entered my office and sat on the couch, Robin and Jim looked like children dragged into the principal's office. They hadn't followed through on their commitment to do the therapeutic exercises between sessions I'd recommended for them. They weren't defensive or blaming each other, just disappointed that yet again they hadn't done their part to move therapy forward in this way.

"Listen," I said with a smile. "You're not the only clients who struggle to get homework done. In fact, part of the point of asking you to do homework is to help you learn to change routines and behaviors on your own. My wife and I have been doing these homework exercises for decades. They work really well to help us strengthen our relationship, and we still have long lapses where we can't find the time to do them. So how about I offer you my carrot-and-stick approach?"

They looked intrigued.

"Here's the deal," I continued.

"If you do your homework as agreed on, I'll give you the next session for free. That's the carrot–and the added bonus is more success in therapy. But if you don't, then in addition to paying for the next session, you'll have to give an equal amount of money to my favorite charity. That's the stick. And obviously, I am not personally going to take your money because I would hate to be profiting by your failure."

Robin immediately turned to Jim and exclaimed, "A free session! We can do this!" And indeed they did. Although I was out a chunk of change the next week, I was delighted, because even though the initial effort was the result of a fun bribe, it led them to continue following through with their homework, hence continued improvement in their relationship.

Over the years, the couples in my practice who've actually done homework exercises have reported communicating better and being more affectionate and more supportive of each other than couples who haven't. Doing communication homework tasks has led to more careful listening to each other in general. Doing physical-affection exercises has led to more spontaneous gestures of affection. And changes in behavior and interactions that couples have made on their own at home have increased their sense of competence, self-esteem, and positive feelings about each other and the relationship. In fact, the implementation of homework is the single variable that predicates successful treatment in my couple therapy.

For much of my career, however, I'd been like too many couple therapists who assign exercises between sessions, giving the homework more as an afterthought than as the first priority of couple therapy. I'd throw out a few ideas at the end of a session, couples frequently wouldn't do them, and sometimes the next week I wouldn't even remember what I'd suggested. In general, I simply wasn't good at motivating couples to do homework. And when they didn't do it, I was reluctant to start each session dealing with their excuses and feeling like a scold or a school principal. In many ways, I was just as resistant to dealing with homework as my clients were, and my own antipathy to pushing homework prevented me from seeing why couples have difficulty doing it–and why it's so important.

Why Therapy Homework Is Difficult

Most couples, I discovered when I started to ask, say their difficulty in doing the homework is because of time pressure, but underneath the "we don't have time" excuse are more difficult matters. By the time couples have arrived in my office, they've developed deeply ingrained habits and patterns of interaction that allow them to coexist and function together while holding deep feelings of ambivalence, hurt, distrust, and sometimes anger with each other. They've already made countless efforts to improve their relationship on their own, so most of them feel that they've been there, done that—and have failed repeatedly.

Instead of labeling a couple's difficulties with doing homework as a problem or resistance, I now see it as an opportunity for them to explore their resistant feelings safely, normalize difficulties with change, and help them choose homework that they can and want to do. Exploring problems with doing homework also allows me to help each partner take responsibility for his or her own behavior rather than blaming each other.

Once I realized these benefits, I made a full commitment to encourage couples to prioritize doing homework as the core of our couple work. To make sure I'm successful in motivating them, I use what I call the Six Ps:

- Preparation
- Planning
- Practicing
- Processing
- Pushing
- Perpetuating

Preparation

Starting with the initial discussion with the couples who choose the skill-building behavioral approach, I convey how the work done between sessions is the key to success. I explain that I don't always schedule weekly sessions because I expect that couples will be working hard to build their competence and confidence in their relationship through the assignments at home. I explicitly say that engagement with homework is essential to success.

Planning

I don't simply give homework assignments; I want couples to come up with their own homework or choose from a menu of possibilities. No matter what they decide, it's critical that the choice be collaborative. When it comes to homework, one size definitely doesn't fit all, and the more the partners collaborate in choosing and designing their homework, the more they'll feel ownership and investment in its success.

I ask couples to place the same priority on doing homework that they place on showing up for an appointment with me–which can be a big challenge in the hurly-burly of everyday life. Even small assignments, like a communication exercise that only takes fifteen minutes twice a week, is hard for people to schedule and follow through with. So it's essential for each partner to make a commitment to prioritize the effort.

In fact, having each partner take responsibility for his or her actions is at the core of almost all successful couple therapy, and this is a good way to get that momentum started.

Practicing

For homework to succeed, it's critical for couples to practice in the room with me so they can experience how to do a task with coaching from me. Then I'll often step out of the room to have them practice on their own to solidify their sense of ownership and competence without me.

When working with intimacy and sexuality issues, for example, I help couples practice an exercise called "Loving Fingers—Hurt and Angry Feelings." Couples take turns giving each other a light shoulder massage while I encourage them to internally experience their negative, hurt, resistant, angry, distrusting feelings. This helps them learn to touch each other lovingly while acknowledging that they have a mess of mixed feelings. I might cap that session by stepping out of the room so they can give each other a hug and experience the power of that touch while also allowing themselves to have difficult, uncomfortable feelings. Of course, some couples (or one partner) may feel unready to do this, but that allows me to address the importance of being able to say no and to adjust the pace of our work.

Processing

We always start the next session by deciding and discussing what aspects of the homework worked and what didn't. Having each partner held accountable for his or her own actions around homework breaks patterns, reveals resistance, and short-circuits the blame game. If one partner is compliant and the other isn't, I can bring affectionate curiosity—not judgment or blame—to the feelings blocking them from fully participating. Often this allows the therapy to go deeper into the underlying pain and vulnerability that lies beneath the surface for the couple.

Sometimes a couple reports that they did their homework but didn't like or it didn't help. That's always a welcome opportunity to explore with greater depth and refinement what they believe would help that they feel ready to try. Again, creating successful homework is a collaborative creation by the couple and the therapist as a team.

Pushing

I'm as persistent as a dog chewing on a bone when helping couples do homework. I ask them to write down the homework task, or I send them an email restating it. I ask them to call or write to me if they have questions or if it's not happening. With couples who really struggle to follow through with homework, like Robin and Jim, sometimes I'll even offer an incentive and/or a penalty to get them started. I've also gone so far as to recommend that the couple take a break from treatment until they're able to do agreed-upon homework.

Perpetuating

I celebrated my fiftieth wedding anniversary last December. Over the years, my dear wife and I, her relentless therapist husband, have been practicing many of the homework assignments I routinely give my clients. But do we practice what I preach about making them our first priority? No. We often lapse, forget, and disregard our relationship practices, even though we know they're highly effective. So we often have to rededicate ourselves to the work. The simple truth is that with all self-discipline practices, like meditation and physical exercise, homework practices are difficult to sustain. Thus, toward the end of successful therapy, when couples are doing well with their homework, we space out sessions progressively, with the understanding that they need to keep up their homework between our intermittent sessions. In many instances, that leads to twice-a-year or once-a-year sessions before we consider the therapy complete. Couples prepare for the possibility that they'll lapse and discuss how they'll get back on track. They accept that it'll always take maintenance.

Clients often have a hard time with the core truth of what it takes to be a successful couple: hard work that never ends. It's not always about the therapeutic breakthroughs, the dramatic insights, the tenderness of amends and forgiveness. Just like cultivating a successful garden, you can't enjoy the fruits of your labor without putting in the effort of weeding and nourishing the soil, day in and day out, decade after decade. But rather than brush this truth aside, we therapists can help couples accept and practice this, with the aim of continuously nourishing their relationship long after therapy ends.

4

HOMEWORK THAT WORKS WELL FOR MY CLIENTS

"Well, I would like Jim to be my love slave for one hour on Saturday," Carla said with a twinkle in her eye.

Jim first looked startled and then very curious.

"Slow down there, Jim," said Carla, enjoying her own joke. "I don't mean anything kinky." She turned back to me. "What I would like Jim to do for me is to move the furniture around in the living room so we can check whether we want to rearrange anything, and I also would like him to dust all the high shelves I can't reach because he's much taller than me, and I would like him to put away the big stack of books next to his bed that he keeps saying he'll put away. I think that will take about an hour."

"What do you think, Jim? Sounds like Carla thinks this would be pretty hot stuff," I said, going along with the joke.

"Well, whatever floats her boat, Doc. I'm in."

I call this the "Tender Loving Care" homework. If couples choose the behavioral change pathway, this is one of four different exercises that couples consider trying right from the start of the treatment.

I want to share each of them with you in depth with examples because the devil is in the details. I offer two possibilities around communication, one around managing conflict safely, one that builds negotiation skills, and one around nurturing/effortful love behavior like the opening example.

The key to success is that couples choose their homework together, and less is actually more. I may give couples two or three choices in the session, but I strongly encourage them to only choose as much as they are sure they can do. Doing one exercise well and consistently is much more effective than trying and failing to do more.

The Talk/Listen Exercise

Many couple therapists utilize the active listening format originally created by Carl Rogers back in the 1950s. That model evolved into a key element of parent effectiveness training in the 1970s and then was popularized in couple therapy, particularly by the Imago Relationship Therapy model developed by Harville Hendrix and Helen Hunt in the 1990s.

However, the way I help couples with active listening is quite different from other models. I don't emphasize either careful speaking (for example, using "I" statements) or empathic listening. I help folks focus on accurate reflection of the words as a way of staying focused and managing their reactivity.

Here's the handout I give couples. We first discuss the exercise, and then I have them practice in the room with me.

***

Rules for the Talk/Listen Exercise

One person talks about whatever they want to for fifteen minutes. Every minute or two the listener reflects back as accurately as possible what the talker is saying without judgment, rebuttal, or any other editorial comment, not even a positive one. The listener contains their reactivity as best they can. The talker can correct the listener if they feel the listener is missing the main points.

There should be two scheduled sessions of only fifteen minutes per week with a minimum of twenty-four hours between sessions. There should be no comment on what the talker discussed except in the talk/listen format.

Please remember that this clunky communication exercise is simply designed to allow each member of a couple to discuss difficult and vulnerable feelings in a safe manner. It is neither a decision-making nor a problem-solving technique. Don't judge the value of the exercise on whether it makes you feel closer in the moment. Frequently, it won't.

***

Katie and Bill were quite eager to get started with behavioral change and skill building, and we started with the Talk/Listen (T/L) exercise.

"So, you two, this exercise is really focused on hearing your partner accurately and feeding their own words back to them. Most folks tend to show understanding by paraphrasing what someone says in their own words. This exercise isn't normal communication. Concentrating on accurately mirroring back your partner's words keeps you from feeling defensive reactive. It also helps you keep listening well even if part of you feels like jumping in and debating. The focused mirroring-back of your partner's words is a little bit like paying attention to the breath when meditating—it keeps you focused. And the other key point is that literally none of us get listened to very carefully in our lives. When we hear our own words coming back to us, we have an opportunity to really consider if we're saying exactly what we mean to be saying.

"Let's just try this for a bit. So you can get the feel of it. You both need to come up with something to say. It doesn't have to be heavy duty. This is just practice, but the person who goes second can't respond to the person going first. Each of you needs to have some thought about what you want to say because I don't want it to be a dialogue just yet. We're looking for two separate monologues to start."

They both paused, and then Katie jumped in and said, "You go first, Bill. I always do all the talking."

We looked at Bill, who was hesitant. "Would that be okay, Bill?" I asked gently. "It doesn't have to be heavy."

"Usually she finds something wrong with whatever I say."

Suddenly, I was at a choice point. Do we go into Bill's painful feelings or stay focused on practicing the exercise? More often than not, since

I am trying to help couples manage difficult feelings rather than be overwhelmed by them, I will keep encouraging them to stay with the exercise.

"So, Bill, you could choose to talk with her about those feelings, and Katie, you would have to play by the rules and discuss something else, and also don't hit him over the head on the car ride home," I said with smile.

"I promise I won't get on his case later," she said reluctantly.

"Great, Katie, are you ready with something to say?"

She nodded.

"Okay, Bill you're up."

Bill shifted uncomfortably in his seat and looked at me.

"Go ahead and look at her. And Katie, I'll let you know when to repeat what he says. It will feel quite weird at first."

"Well, I really want this to work out, but I feel like you're always disappointed in me. Like I don't measure up. I feel like you're always frustrated with me and—"

"Hold on, Bill that's a lot. Can you feed that back, Katie?"

She paused and then started a little haltingly, "So I hear you saying that you want to work this out, but that I am always disappointed in you and that you're not good enough, and that I am always mad at you."

"Great listening, Katie. He did say 'frustrated,' not 'mad,' but you mostly got all of it well." I turned back to Bill. "Keep going, Bill. This is a good start."

***

And we're off. The essence of this exercise is that both members of the couple get to experience that there can be room for their individual feelings in the relationship. The speaker isn't asked to speak in therapeutic "I" position language, but to speak from the heart, which often can come across as critical and harsh. None of us know how to listen to criticism easily, and it's a skill to learn how to contain one's reactive feelings while feeling attacked. The value of the twenty-four-hour rule is for the couples to be able to practice this containment in their relationship while doing everyday life.

Sometimes when couples are anxious that the exercise might get too aggressive, I encourage them to start using the T/L format but not talking about their relationship, just the other parts of their lives.

For couples who seem really ready to utilize the format for truly difficult issues, I might tell them a pretty extreme story from my own relationship to give them a sense of how powerful it can be. My clients are usually intrigued when I do careful self-disclosure from my own marriage. Done well, a little sense of the therapist's humaneness in relationships can be very helpful.

At the end of the session with Katie and Bill, I said, "So, would you guys like to hear a pretty over-the-top story of how this exercise has worked in my own marriage?"

Katie and Bill nodded in unison.

"My wife and I do most of the exercises I will be offering you, but like most couples, we have difficulty being disciplined, and months can go by without us practicing what I preach.

"Back when the kids were little, Kate (that's my wife) and I were having a lot of conflict about how to include religious training and church in their lives. We were really disagreeing and managing poorly with bickering, angry silence, and emotional distancing."

"Finally, I said, 'Honey, maybe we should do the T/L exercise about this stuff.' To which she said, 'Screw your exercise.'"

Bill and Katie laughed.

"Yeah, I know, it's not always easy to be married to a therapist. Anyway, she finally reluctantly agreed, and it certainly made sense to me that she go first.

"So did I show up for this exercise as my normal kind, calm, and compassionate therapist self? Of course not. I was agitated and tense. My eyes were little beady slits. My jaws were clenched, and I was grasping my knees so hard that my knuckles were white. She knew I was mad, and she was just as mad.

"She began, and soon I had to feed back to her the following: 'So I hear you saying that you've always known that I am a narcissist, but you are shocked that I could be so selfish at the expense of our kids' well-being.'

"To which she responded, 'Right!' and then she had fourteen more minutes of things to say. Then the alarm went off, and we were done.

"Now I had to wait twenty-four hours before I could respond, and we were just ships passing in the night with me glimpsing at my watch nonstop and rehearsing my turn to let her have it.

"Sure enough, twenty-four hours later I tattooed her back for fifteen minutes, and she listened to me just as impeccably as I had listened to her while being just as angry.

"Again, we broke it off without continuing the conflict. We each got thoroughly heard well even though we still completely disagreed.

"The next day we were in the kitchen doing the banal chore of putting away groceries together. The atmosphere was almost normal, and then my wife said in a funny, almost begrudging sort of way, 'So I guess it's good we talked.'

"It made me laugh because we had obviously gotten nowhere with the exercise, but I said, 'You know what, we can't work this out on our own. We're going to have to get help.' And we agreed on that.

"And the next night, we could go to the movies even though we still had our huge problem. We had shared our feelings, played within the rules carefully, agreed to disagree, and then chosen an action plan. That Friday night, we both reached for each other's hand."

"I don't know if we're ready for that, Dr. Treadway," said Bill, who looked a little alarmed.

"Yeah, I know. That's an extreme example, and my wife and I have been at this marriage business for fifty years. Believe me, it's an acquired skill. I could tell you a whole bunch of way less successful stories, but that's enough for today."

***

What I really like about this exercise is that it allows couples to hold deep, hard disagreements without getting swept away by their huge emotional volatility. Having a safe way of critiquing, disagreeing, and complaining to one's partner actually operates a little like the whistle on a teakettle. The couple can blow off steam on a regular basis before the build-up of pressure becomes dangerous. (Obviously Kate and I, in our parenting conflict, should have done the exercise several months sooner.) When couples do the exercise on a regular, scheduled basis, they learn to feel collaborative and competent in having a protocol for dealing with conflict. Couples learn how to hold their divisive issues together, and it actually strengthens their sense of being a successful team. Finally, when each member feels like their partner can really listen to them and pay attention, they tend to go beyond the "bitch and moan" sessions to more tender and intimate sharing of emotions such as feeling sad that one of them can't connect with one of their children, or feeling like they're becoming a has-been at work, or even fear of getting old and sick and dying.

One couple called it "sacred listening," and they had a ritual in which she made a circle of stones she had gathered on countless New England beaches. She then put two comfy pillows in the center of the circle, and they stepped together holding hands into their sacred silence.

I always start couples in this spare and simple T/L exercise rather than the more complex, interactive dialogues that many therapists use. However, once couples learn how to follow the format and do it at home successfully, there many variants that can really be useful. Here are some examples:

1) Interactive T/Ls. One member of a couple talks for three to five timed minutes while the other actively listens, and then they switch with the understanding that the second member of the couple has the freedom to talk about whatever they want to talk about. They can respond to what their partner says or start on an entirely different topic. Communication is often a subtle form of power struggle in which there is a covert competition about whose agenda is running the conversation. By having each member of the couple free to use their time however they want, they create a sense of spaciousness and freedom in their conversation that is actually quite startling. Couples usually agree that they will do three turns each. It is essential that once the eighteen minutes of back and forth is over that they don't continue the conversation for at least twenty-four hours.
2) Empathic summary. At the end of a T/L, the listener makes a summary of what they have heard and expresses empathy and compassion for their partner. This is not easy, and we practice in the therapy room how to express empathy and compassion well, even while having other, more difficult and reactive feelings.
3) Spontaneous T/Ls. Once couples are doing T/Ls well, it's possible for one member to request a formal T/L (taking fifteen-minute turns spaced out by twenty-four hours) or an interactive timed T/L on the spot. This technique can frequently nip conflict in the bud.

4) Improved listening. Not surprisingly, couples who use the T/L method commonly report they are simply listening to each other in regular, every day communication. Which is, after all, the point!

The Time-Out Rule

Most couple therapists have a way of stopping a raging argument with some kind of time-out rule. Unfortunately, it frequently doesn't work because the person being silenced by the time-out often feels controlled or abandoned by the person who is trying to stop the conflict. I have more failures than I can count by acting like a referee in the middle of a prizefight trying to pull boxers apart. No wonder couples can't do it well on their own.

However, in recent years I have developed the Time-Out Rule, which really works if I can get couples to do it (and that is hard work).

Here's what I say to a couple.

"So if either of you want to stop an escalating conflict, you can 'ask' for a time out. Your partner has to 'give' it to you, and in return, he or she has to come back to you within twelve hours and say, 'Thank you for the time out. Would you like to have the last word?' Then your partner gets an extra five minutes of T/L to finish their thoughts while you actively listen. You can't restart the fight by rebutting, and you have to wait for your own regularly scheduled T/L to respond to your partner if you want to."

This technique works well because the time out is requested and appreciated, and the person who is stopped actually feels the respect of being able to finish their thoughts at the initiation of the person who stopped the conflict in the first place. This method makes ending conflict a reciprocal and collaborative effort.

What makes it difficult is that the person who is given the time-out often doesn't remember or "forgets" to come back with the gratitude and offer for the last word, and without that reciprocal gesture the whole thing collapses like a fallen souffle.

However, for some couples the fear and panic that they are feeling in the conflict can make them feel controlled and abandoned by their partner when they invoke the Time Out Rule in the heat of the conflict. As one woman said. "He uses the rule to gag me."

It is extremely important to help both members of the couple use tools like the progressive relaxation response technique (the tensing and releasing of muscle groups in synch with deep breathing) or getting into a sequence of yoga postures, or utilizing some meditative mantras to calm themselves down.

For some highly reactive volatile couples, unless they can learn how to manage their intense feelings skillfully, the Time Out Rule won't work. it is essential to teach them self-calming skills in sessions and to have them practice these skills at home when they are not in an aroused state in order for them to be able to use these techniques when they are in a fully agitated flight/fight emotional state.

Couples in my practice are always inventing variations on my homework that are frequently wonderful. For example, Ben and Sam were delighted with themselves when Ben reported to me, "We didn't think your idea worked well for us. We added the Three-Strikes-and-You're-Out Rule, which works for us. One of us takes a time-out for five minutes and then we try again, and then if we need another TO, it's for fifteen minutes and then we try again, and then if that doesn't work, we'll do your complicated thing with waiting for twelve hours and then the last word stuff. How about that, David? You can use it with your other clients, too."

And I do.

"The Business of Business Is Business" Decision-Making Tool

Being a modern couple with unclear role definitions for who does what with whom and when about virtually every dimension of life leaves couples in nonstop negotiations, which drowns out the sparks of intimacy, sexiness, and romance that most couples yearn for. So, couples need to learn how to negotiate well, make decisions together, and compromise without letting it be a test of their love and caring for each other. That's why I call this "The Business of Business Is Business." I often say to couples, "Just treat stuff as a necessary part of the job of being a small business. Keep it fair, and don't take it too personally. It isn't a test of your love or relationship."

I teach them some basic notions about how to have a business meeting, which include having agreed-upon agendas, observing time limits, taking turns, and ending with clarity about agreements, as well as who will do what and by when. I also encourage them to use the following handout for making decisions.

The Decision-Making Protocol

1) Identify the issue to be decided (any issue from something small, like whether to stay in or go out tonight, or medium, like summer vacations and holidays, to large, such as having another child, making a career change, or buying a house.) I usually encourage couples to practice on exceedingly small issues first.
2) Think through your own needs and desires on the issue separate from considering what your partner might want. I call it "thinking selfishly first." Usually one member of the couple begins with what seems to them like a reasonable compromise without articulating their own needs. This often backfires in the negotiations because one person has already begun with a compromise proposal and may not feel that's it fair to have to compromise more.
3) Express your wishes in the Talk/Listen format, explaining what you want and why. The partner actively listens and then states what they originally wanted and why rather than responding or debating what was said by the person who went first.

   It doesn't matter how far apart you are at the beginning. It is very important to have your wants known fully so that when compromises are made, both partners can see how much each of them has stretched.
4) Separate for a short time (even if it's just a matter of minutes on a small issue) to think about what each partner has proposed, and then come out with what you feel is a fair compromise on the two positions.
5) Then meet again and propose your compromise ideas to each other, and see if you can't compromise the compromise proposals into a hybrid that will work for both of you.
6) Often it will become apparent that any compromise will tilt toward one partner or another. Frequently folks get stuck there. If it's not clear who is going to give in. So pause and rate on a 0–10 scale how much it matters to you to get the compromise more your way. The rating frequently reveals that one partner really cares a lot more, and that makes it easier for the other to be gracious and generous and get the credit for being so. For example, if Marni cares a nine about getting her position and Harry only cares a five, then it makes

sense for Harry to "gift" it to Marni. She gets to feel given to, and Harry gets to feel appreciated. Obviously, in some couples one person always cares more about getting their way, which becomes a discussion point in their therapy.

7) There are several obvious ways of compromising. Certainly gifting is a highly effective way for couples to resolve an issue. Gifting is not based on winning and losing or right-versus-wrong debating, but on relational generosity and appreciation. When both members of the couple feel equally strongly, then "back scratching" or taking turns can be proposed. This is where one of you gives in on the particular issue and proposes a reciprocal turn on an equivalent issue, such as agreeing to stay in this Saturday night as long as the other person agrees to go out next Saturday night.

***

Here's an example of using the Decision-Making Tool. Peter and Ellen, who were struggling with Peter's drinking, negotiated in my office that it would be okay for him to drink until our next session using his own standard for what constitutes safe, responsible use of alcohol. And in return, Ellen asked that he be willing to negotiate mutually arrived-upon ground rules for alcohol use if she was uncomfortable with how he was using alcohol.

Despite it sounding a little flip, I also suggest to couples that they consider a coin toss. Frequently the process of actually making the decision does more relational harm than whatever the actual decision is. Helping couples learn how to defer to each other with something as arbitrary as a coin flip teaches them the importance of being able to take turns and tolerate not getting their way. At least on small decisions, this is often very useful.

Ben and Sam, the same couple who created their own Time Out Rule guidelines, also came up with what they called "Keeping Score," which is keeping a running tally of who was getting their way on decisions. They weren't trying to be compulsively 50–50, but it did help them, in a friendly way, to keep track of the fairness balance over time.

Finally, on major issues like the difficulty my wife and I had deciding on our children's religious upbringing, seeking a consultation or a third-party arbitration can be critically important, as it proved to be for us.

This Decision-Making Tool helps couples become competent and confident about their negotiating skills. Since negotiating is a relentlessly frequent activity in couple relationships, becoming good at it gives couples a strong boost to their relational self-esteem and their sense of being a collaborative partnership.

Tender Loving Care

Grooming behavior seen in our primate ancestry suggests needing to be nurtured doesn't end with childhood. We all need attention and nurturing and being taken care of in our grown-up lives. We are so busy in our lives, often nobody in a couple gives or receives nurturing and undivided attention. I teach my couples to prioritize taking turns giving and receiving, whether that has to do with communication, sex, affection, or affirmation. I call it "two of you paying attention to one of you at a time."

I remember my wife, the very busy physician, and I, the very busy clinician, would often have an end-of-the-day competition describing how hard our days were. Clearly, we were competing for attention, but instead we got into exhausting, unlistened-to whining. After ten years of this (change can be slow), one of us said, "Why don't we take turns?" So when Monday night was her night, I could show up in my most engaged, professional, and caring manner and say, "Honey, tell me all about your day." And I'd mean it, because Tuesday night she would do the same for me . . . and when the good Dr. Kate is focused on listening well, one literally feels bathed in loving attention. It was like someone waved a magic wand, and our day's end became sweet and tender rather than filled with feisty bickering.

Here is the handout for this exercise.

TLC

We all need to be nurtured and made to feel special from time to time in our relationships. Too often we are under appreciated and taken for granted. Gifting is a way for couples to make sure that each week they each take a little time to give some tender loving care to their partner.

Key ingredients:

1) Each partner comes up with his or her own very specific gift and negotiates a time when they can get it.
2) The gift is behavioral and time limited, like breakfast in bed, back rubs, a special chore, favor, or treat, etc.
3) Neither partner has to be "in the mood" to give or receive. Just practice giving and receiving as best you can.
4) Giver gives without expectations of gratitude, and receiver doesn't have to make sure giver feels good.
5) Learn to do this practice for a while before applying this idea to sexual gifting (that's the advanced course),

***

Couples learn to clearly negotiate behavioral and reciprocal gifts. One can't ask for their partner to be nicer. And one can't ask for their partner to drive the kids to school every day when the other partner asked for a fifteen-minute back rub. Couples often have some difficulty coming up with ideas, although women are frankly much quicker than men to generate a list of possibilities (especially when sex is taken off the table).

People can choose anything that is doable as long as the partner can say no. I don't remember how long ago I started using the odd saying "The Road to Yes Begins in the Village of No," but it is incredibly important for couples to learn how to say no well and receive no well as part of learning how to say yes to each other.

I often give clients of examples of what other couples come up with, like when I described the exercise to Bill and Katie.

"So, one husband who was on a restricted diet asked that his wife cook steak and baked potatoes with lots of butter and sour cream. At first she balked for health reasons, and then she got why this could feel like such a gift to him. As long as it would be only an occasional request, she could give it. Another example was a woman who asked her husband to come to bed a half-hour earlier one night a week and read out loud from her favorite childhood book, *The Secret Garden*. And he somewhat sheepishly asked that she draw a bubble bath for him and then wash his hair. That was incredibly sweet. And I remember one guy who was having a lot of difficulty coming up with an idea, and he finally asked for his wife to greet him at the door one night a week with a beer, his slippers, the newspaper, and the TV clicker so he could go into the TV room for an hour before engaging with the family. At first she got mad and said, 'Are you kidding? Here we are supposedly working on improving our relationship, and you just want to watch TV by yourself?' But she was a very smart woman, and within a few seconds she calmed right down and said, 'Well, if you really recognize that this is a gift and you give me mine (she had asked for him to spend an hour gardening with her), I guess I can do it." And she did. And it really mattered to him.'

"So, Bill and Katie, what do you each think you would want for a gift this coming week?"

***

My wife and I have worked on all of these ideas and homework assignments ourselves over the years. (And it's much easier to "preach" rather than "practice.") But there was one point when we were struggling with my life-threatening cancer that our hard work really paid off.

It was the end of a long afternoon of me, sick as a dog from cancer and chemo, watching the Red Sox game. My wife came home from work and started telling me about a meeting with a patient of hers who was dying of my kind of cancer. She was near tears describing the meeting with him and his wife and kids.

In that moment, I knew she needed me to rally, but I just couldn't. I said, "Listen honey, I can't go there with you right now. Let me just watch the end of this stupid game and then I will be able to focus. I just can't. Can we wait?"

Kate was startled, but she really heard me and said, "Okay, we'll talk later."

I felt so nurtured by her ability to accept my limitations that when the game was over, I went and found her and was able to take her in my arms and let her weep about having just experienced the "good-bye" session that she anticipated we would have with our children. In that exchange, we both felt heard and held.

The essence of all these exercises is to help couples learn how to skillfully make empathic room for each other's feelings and to treat each with love and compassion.

Not surprisingly, I find myself reading the framed quote I have on my desk to a lot of couples.

> Be kind,
> for everyone you meet
> is fighting a great battle.
>
> Phyllo of Alexandria, 1st century AD

5

BEHIND CLOSED DOORS

The Intimacy/Sexuality Conundrum

They were a Mutt-and-Jeff couple I'd been seeing for a while. She was petite, and he was at least six-five. They actually had a good relationship, but their sex life had evaporated. I was giving them my seduction/rejection homework.

"So, each of you practices making a flirtatious overture while the other finds a way of saying 'No, thank you' in an affirming, positive way. Believe it or not almost no one knows how to say 'no' well to a sexual advance."

"I know how I would say 'no' well," Sonya said in her husky Belgian accent. "I would go up close to John, stand on my tiptoes, and I would put one arm around his neck, and then I would place my other hand lightly on his crotch. Then I would say, 'Oh, darling, I would love to make love to you tonight. But I had such a wretched day, I know it couldn't be all we would want it to be. But this is your rain check. Then I would give his private parts a gentle squeeze.'"

John looked at me, and I looked at him wide-eyed. I couldn't wait to tell my wife, Kate, a new way to say "No, thank you."

As most couples transition from the romantic sexuality and intimacy of the "in love" experience to the humdrum journey of learning how to negotiate differences in everyday life, the power and allure, joy and intensity of romantic intimacy inevitably begin to dim. Giving and receiving sexual favors are often tangled up in negotiations and power struggles. Most couple therapists assume that if they improve the quality of a couple's relationship in terms of conflict management, friendliness, cooperation, then sexual intimacy will improve on its own. This is often not true. Couples frequently need help in rekindling their sexuality no matter how much their relationship has improved.

I often ask in first interviews how their difficulties have impacted their sexual life, and that's usually met with some variation of a rueful chuckle, eye roll, or comment like "What sex life?" Even though a couple's presenting problem doesn't mention intimacy and sexuality, those issues are almost always the elephant in the room. I say to clients, "Don't be surprised that making progress in the kitchen won't lead spontaneously to progress in the bedroom. We may need to do some explicit work in that department to get your love life revved up again." Usually couples seem pleased that the issue is on the table and relieved that we're not plunging right on it.

However, sometimes couples present sexuality directly as their reason for being there and sometimes couples bring up sex problems as the real issue that they want to work with after they get comfortable with me. I am quite cautious at moving directly into sexual issues before I have developed a positive comfortable safe relationship with the couple. Even if both members of the couple express a real desire to deal with sexual issues, I usually begin with some of the communication exercises mentioned in the prior chapter. I call it foreplay.

As you will see, working well with couples' intimacy issues involves a lot of emphasis on "effortful love" and learning how to be successfully and happily intimate with each other despite having mixed feelings about their relationship.

Before discussing how best to treat sexuality issues with couples, it's important to step back and consider some of the many challenges that couples face in maintaining a satisfying sexual intimacy in an ongoing, committed relationship. I often give couples the handout below to provide a little psycho-ed about sexuality in our culture, which also helps them feel less shame and failure about their struggles. It really helps couples relax when they understand that their sexual difficulties are actually pretty darn normal.

Why Sustaining a Satisfying Sex Life Is Difficult for Most Couples

A Complicated Side Effect of the Feminist and Sexual Revolutions in the 60s and 70s

Couples' expectations for romantic, mutually satisfying sex lives have sky rocketed. Now that women feel appropriately entitled to their own sexual satisfaction, it puts pressure on both both partners to be better lovers. The increased expectations for sex to fulfill romantic and intimacy needs tends to create performance anxiety for both men and women alike.

Societal Sexual Saturation

In our culture, we are literally bombarded with sexually stimulating images all the time on TV, movies, ads, magazines, and other media. Just pick up *Cosmopolitan* in the supermarket line and look at the one-hundred new techniques that will supposedly send you are over the moon. Meanwhile, pornography is the most viewed material online. And virtually all the sex that is portrayed is with impeccably beautiful, buff, Photoshopped men and women with impossibly perfect bodies. This intimidates, overwhelms, and challenges normal folks about what is sexy enough. Everyone tends to think that everyone else is having great sex, when in reality there's an epidemic of couples barely having sex at all behind their closed doors.

Negotiating Normal Differences in Levels of Sexual Desire

When people first fall in love, they are so eager to be pleasing to each other that they rarely acknowledge to themselves or each other any sexual incompatibilities, and when they are dating they tend to initiate sexual encounters mutually and easily. However, as couples settle into their routines, the other commitments of everyday living tend to take precedence. That's when some of the normal difference in usual male and female sex drives begin to create tension around how much sex is good enough, and then the issue of how does sexuality get negotiated well is the huge challenge. People tend to become either routinized into schedules or into low-risk negotiations like this,

"You wanna? Later?"
"Are you kidding after the day I had?"

This kind of exchange is not the stuff of Hallmark cards, but it manages to help people not hurt each other's their feelings too much. In some ways it's easier to initiate a romantic encounter with a stranger in a bar than with your bedmate of thirty years. It's difficult to reject your partner's romantic advances in a positive, affirming way.

All Roads Don't Lead to Rome

Each individual has their own pathway to sexual arousal and intimate connection. The traditional divide was that most men seemed to think sex was the best pathway to intimacy while most women needed to feel intimate before becoming sexual. However, as gender clichés are breaking down, the variability of sexual desires and level of frequency are also evolving. It is much more common for women to be wanting more sex then men nowadays, which is particularly painful for both genders. It's always been difficult for the person wanting more frequency to ask and get frequent rejections and the person wanting less frequency to always be in the role of rejecter while feeling pressure to engage in order to be a good spouse. This is even more painful when it's not reflecting traditional gender rules. Being a woman pursuing a man for sex feels terrible because she takes it intensely personally that the man is not into her. A man who is withdrawing from sex can feel unmanly and inadequate and anxious.

Unfulfilling Sexual Experience

The reality of sexual intensity and satisfaction waning with familiarity is well known. Premature ejaculation, difficulty achieving orgasm or erections, and lack of desire can lead to a cycle of disappointing encounters and a tendency to experience sex as a job rather than a joy.

Everyday Life Is Not an Aphrodisiac

Conflict and stress, kids and work add to the diminishment of time and opportunity for romantic feelings. It's difficult for a mom to feel sexually interested in her husband if he was an hour late picking up their three-year-old at daycare. Often couples try to have sex by shutting out the difficult issues of the day, retreating into their own erotic fantasy world where the bodies are new, hot, young, and exciting and the action is an adventure. This is a fine solution for creating arousal, but it often means couples aren't really connecting to each other relationally, so the experience doesn't necessarily feel very intimate or rewarding. Making love can end up feeling more like masturbation.

Masturbation and Porn

Since virtually any sexually arousing image can be turned on with the flick of a finger on one's computer or phone, accessing easy stimulation and relief is available all the time. More and more frequently men and women are turning to pornography along with reliable sex toys as a way of satisfying their sexual needs easily and efficiently rather than turning toward their partner with all the human complexities, negotiations, challenges that two-person sex entails.

***

George and Joan had made a lot of progress in their couple therapy in communicating better, making decisions collaboratively, and enjoying each other's company more. However, these positive steps had not led to more intimacy in the bedroom. Their sex life had waned significantly after their ten-year-old was born, and at this point they were having perfunctory, unrewarding sex about once a month. They were pretty despairing about it and wondered whether the spark was permanently gone. Going over the earlier handout actually reassured them they were normal. Joan had said rather brightly, "Gee, maybe misery does love company. We qualify on almost every point you made."

Now we were ready to start working on enhancing their intimate and sexual life.

"I am afraid that my approach to helping couples rekindle their sexuality is going to sound pretty heavy and unromantic," I started. "I treat a couple's broken-down sex life the same way a surgeon treats a broken leg. You wouldn't say to the patient with the broken leg, 'You need to strengthen that leg by going out for runs,' you would say, 'Well, first we're going to have to reset it, then put it in a cast, and have you be non-weight bearing for a month or so, (you'll need crutches) and then we'll start physical therapy. It might be as much as three months before you'll be running around the tennis court.' Well, that's how we approach healing a couple's sex life."

I paused.

George looked disappointed. Joan looked relieved.

"I know, George, this doesn't sound either romantic or sexy, but it is safe and it is doable, and actually it lays the foundation for having romantic and sexy intimacy down the road."

"Says you, doc," George said with a friendly, teasing smile. "Let's get started."

"So, to start with," I began, "there are four key ingredients to this enterprise: structure, schedule, safety, and choice. We utilize a very specific, spelled-out structure of activities that are scheduled that you'll try regardless of whether or not you're in the "mood" The only goal is that you accomplish the task whether it feels good or not. Most couples who have been hurt and disappointed in their sex life contract and withdraw a little when approaching intimate activity. That's an entirely natural reflex. So, scheduling an intimacy exercise is actually just like the Talk/Listen exercise or Tender Loving Care exercise, which we started with back at the beginning of your therapy.

"It's essential that you guys pick the exercise, and it is also important that if you feel too anxious or agitated that either one of you can say no to doing the exercise when the time comes. I often say when I am teaching this stuff, 'The Road to **Yes** Begins in the Village of **No**.' It's important that doing the exercise isn't forced at the same time you're gently pushing yourselves to overcome your resistance.

"Is this making sense?"

Joan said, "I am glad that you're saying that, Dr. Treadway. It actually will make it easier for me to try if I know I can stop it."

"Sounds like you're giving her a 'Get Out of Jail Free' card," said George.

"Hold on, George, I am sure you don't want her to feel like she's in jail, do you?"

"No, I was just kidding," George said, somewhat defensively.

"I know, and I also know that it really hurts to get rejected a lot. And that it's hard to be trying yet again. You have your own vulnerability and anxiety at play here."

George suddenly looked very sad and just nodded.

This was an important choice point for me. Do I move to the tenderness of his pain and hope to help Joan respond to him with empathy and compassion, or do we keep on going with planning the exercises because letting them get into this conversation might actually set them back into old patterns of blaming and recrimination? When in doubt, ask the couple.

"Let's pause here, George and Joan. It seems like this a vulnerable moment for both of you, and we could open it up so that perhaps you could really appreciate each other's tenderness and how scary it is to be trying to address this topic. Or we could keep focusing on planning the next steps while acknowledging that this tenderness will be there over and over again as you try to become more intimately connected. Which do you think would be better?"

A long pause followed.

"I think we should keep going," said Joan. "We've talked and talked about all this, and I think we need to focus on trying things. I know George doesn't really think that I want our intimate life to change, but I do."

George looked surprised and pleased. "I would say ditto to that."

"Well, let's try moving forward, and we'll check back in and see how this is feeling by the end of the session," I said.

"I usually give couples three choices of exercises or a chance to come up with their own exercise. Which would you prefer?"

"Please give us your ideas," Joan said.

"Okay, you could start by taking turns with a half-hour back massage. Or you could do a three minute make-out session where you kiss and hug and caress each other on the sofa with clothes on and stop when the alarm goes off. Or you could take a shower together and take turns soaping each other up for three minutes."

They both looked a little uncomfortable.

"The key here is that there is no right choice. Whatever you choose will be right."

Joan looked immediately less tense and said, "I know George might want to do more, but I think starting with the back massage is the safest bet for me."

"That's what I thought you would say," George said with some disappointment. "But I guess we have to start somewhere."

"Yes, that's true, George, but what would you have picked?"

"I thought the shower idea sounded pretty hot. That would have been my choice."

"Why don't you two discuss it?"

They looked at each other shyly.

George said, "I think it will work better if we start with what you want."

Joan seemed very grateful and said, "I am sorry that I'm not ready for the shower thing. I would be so embarrassed. I'm so fat."

"You look good to me, honey," George said with a sweet smile.

At the end of the session, I offered them the following **Tips** homework sheet for them to consider for next steps, which I said we would discuss when they came back for the next session.

***

Tips for the Art and Comedy, the Magic and Frustration of Sexual Intimacy

Ways to Talk

I'll Tell You Mine; You Tell Me Yours

This technique encourages couples to share, either in or out of the office, their earliest experiences (both good and bad) of their own gender, family-of-origin attitudes around sexuality, puberty, their own earliest sexual feelings, romantic feelings, and adolescent experimentation with love and sex.

Loving Fingers/Hurt and Angry Feelings

This exercise is one I usually do in my office. Each member of the couple takes turns giving and then receiving a gentle neck massage with their eyes closed while simultaneously allowing themselves to experience their full range of feelings, including resistance, fear, hurt, and anger. This technique helps them accept that they may have ambivalent and even negative feelings while touching each other and being closer.

Bedtime Reading

Couples read books on sexuality and intimacy which can provide a much greater sense of erotic possibilities and experiments. Couples may also choose to read or look at erotica or pornography together. This helps couples begin to share their own likes and dislikes in this intimate arena.

Start, Stop, Talk, Start Again

This exercise encourages couples to begin touching and kissing, pause and share their feelings, and then start again. It helps couples stay connected and open with each other while beginning to be sexual.

Grieving the Loss of the Garden of Eden

Virtually all couples have some difficulty transitioning from the "in love" stage of a relationship to the "in life" stage. Usually each member of the couple deals with those feelings alone. Through this exercise, couples learn to share openly their loss of romantic intensity and to grieve the loss of those "in love" feelings together, which can be very tender and intimate.

Love Letters

Couples write some of their favorite sexual or romantic memories of the relationship or write to each other about their own erotic fantasies. This helps couples rekindle some of their old sexual sparks or open more intimately to each other about their private erotic fantasies.

Swish

Using this neuro-linguistic programming (NLP) technique, couples learn to diffuse the build-up of aversive feelings that result from their relationship and/or childhood history by practicing replacing negative imagery with positive imagery.

Things to Do

Traffic Lights

Couples learn to schedule days in the week when they will *not* try to be sexual (red light), days when sex is a possibility (yellow light), and days when some kind of sex is a promise (green light). For many couples it is a great relief to have some nights in the week where there's no pressure or questions about sex.

Tender Loving Care

Couples learn to take turns giving and receiving agreed-upon sexual behavior (gifting). Many couples are held hostage by the tyranny of mutuality, believing it's best if both partners are aroused and have an orgasm. Learning to comfortably give and receive sexual favors takes an enormous amount of pressure off the couple.

The Seduction/Rejection Game

Clients learn how to make sexual advances and rejections in a light, playful and safe manner. One member of the couple is tasked with making flirtatious overtures while the other has to find a flirtatious and loving way of saying "no, thank you."

Swimming Lessons

Clients practice giving and receiving sensual and erotic massages as well as learning to give and receive constructive feedback. This is essentially the type of sensate focus work developed by Masters and Johnson, and is a significant part of sex therapy. I use the term "swimming lessons" to convey that these skill-building exercises are not necessarily that intimate or fun or erotic to start. Almost everyone remembers hating swimming class but wanting to be able to swim.

Little Sexy Encounters

Couples are encouraged to experiment with "making out" behavior in places that are not likely to create pressure to have sex, such as in elevators, cars, or kitchens, and timing a make-out session to last no longer than three minutes. Freeing the couple up from feeling like they have to get aroused and have orgasms also is a pressure reliever.

Masturbation

Couples are invited to experiment with their own masturbatory habits in private and to explore their emotions as they masturbate. Each member of the couple may discover that masturbation can become a greater expression of self-loving and potentially more fulfilling. It may also open up some more intimate feelings about themselves and their sexuality than they might share with each other.

The Art of Mediocrity

This exercise helps couples set lower and less fraught expectations for their sexual encounters in order to relieve their performance pressure. "Ho hum, good enough" sex is as important in a long-term relationship as profoundly connected, intimate sexuality.

***

As we were wrapping up the session, I went over the homework with George and Joan.

"It's important that when you're receiving the massage to feel free to give your partner directions like, 'Use more or less lotion, rub harder or softer, more on this spot,' and those types of directions," I said, "and it's really important for the massager to welcome the instructions. Almost none of us feels comfortable saying how we want to be touched sexually, and most of us have some difficulty being directed. Learning how to give and receive feedback is really important for being good sexual partners. Consider the back massage exercise as a preview of coming attractions," I said as I smiled at them.

George had been glancing at the **Tips** sheet. "Wait a minute, doc. What's this stuff about 'mediocrity'?"

"Good question, George. I am probably the only therapist in the country who goes around espousing the art of mediocrity. One of the biggest things that hurts couples' sexuality is their expectations about how wonderful sex is supposed to be all the time. Let me ask you a question: do you expect every meal to be a gourmet meal?"

"Of course not."

"Right. Most of the time, food is just good enough, nothing special, and actually some of the time kind of mediocre, just fuel. It is really important for you guys to accept that what we're going to be doing here not only won't set off fireworks, but it might not even feel very good, and it could stir up some mix of sad/bad/mad feelings. I don't want you to be afraid or disappointed by that. You know physical therapists are always talking about 'No pain, no gain.' Regaining the ability to make love comfortably and intimately will take time, and it will sometimes make you feel really bad about all the years that you've lost out on since it became difficult.

"Be patient and tender with each other as you start this endeavor. This will take courage and love. And I believe you have it."

After they left, I paused to consider where they were. Clearly George was both engaged and skeptical. And he had some simmering resentment not very far below the surface. Joan was cooperative and compliant but quite anxious, and undoubtedly had her own version of resistance. Perhaps I should have worked more with their feelings when George's sadness showed up in the middle of the session. But Joan's choice to press on was telling. And George was immediately pleased, so it seemed like the right call.

I was glad they'd picked the safer, less sexually focused homework for a start. But I wouldn't be surprised if they had difficulty even scheduling the time to do it. More will be revealed the next time I see them.

How much to push behavioral change and how much to explore and hold the feelings is always a delicate balance in each moment, each session, each therapy from beginning to end. It is the heart and the art of the work.

6

CAMP TREADWAY

Carter and Helen looked tense as they came in for what I call the Camp Treadway Weekend Intensive. We had been working together for a while, and they were having difficulty doing their homework and were discouraged about their progress. The weekend retreat was kind of a doubling down on our therapeutic effort.

After I reviewed the structure of the whole thing, Helen asked anxiously, "What if Carter isn't having a good time?"

"That's exactly the point of the weekend. For Carter to feel free to not have a good time and to be able to share that with you and for you to feel less worried about his feelings and focus more on exploring your own feelings independently. It's not uncommon for one member of the couple to be feeling negatively about the weekend. 'This is terminally hokey,' one guy said when his wife was actually feeling like it was wonderful. The challenge for her was not to let her husband's feelings smother hers. When there's room enough in the couple for both members to have whatever their feelings are, it can feel very spacious and more relaxed for both of you."

"You mean, I'm not supposed to be bothered if he's having a bad time?"

"Well, of course you'll be disappointed, but you don't have to fix it nor do you have to be dependent on his feeling good for you to feel good. And it will be helpful for you to work on appreciating his doing "effortful love," even if he's struggling with it a bit. This is where he gets to see what happens with his feelings as he moves on to another activity and you work on letting go of focusing on his feelings as you move on to the next activity. And you'll discover that actually both of your feelings will shift and change as you move through events.

"Is this making sense?"

"Makes sense to me. She's always trying to make sure I'm okay, and if I'm not then she always thinks that talking about what's wrong is a good plan. She thinks talking about it will make me feel better, and frequently it ends up in argument. Maybe this weekend could be good, after all."

"Okay, guys, let's do the check in that follows each exercise you do and is also at the end of each block. This is the cornerstone of the weekend.

"First, just sit up straight, uncross your legs and close your eyes, then take three deep breaths."

The couple rearranged themselves and began to breathe deeply.

"Now, what I want you do is focus on your body and see what physical experience you are having. Where are you noticing the sensations in your body? Tightness in your chest? Sore knee, backache, butterflies in your stomach? What are you noticing?"

I paused for a moment before continuing. "And now, I want you to focus on what you're feeling, your current emotional state. Keep it simple. One word descriptions: sad, nervous, hopeful, curious, annoyed, skeptical; whatever you are feeling, notice and put it into one or two words. See if you can capture one-word descriptions of your feelings.

"Do each of you know what your bodily sensations are and what in a couple of descriptive words you are feeling?"

They both nodded.

"You go first, Helen. Just open your eyes and say to Carter what bodily feelings you have."

"Well, I'm feeling really fluttery in my chest and belly, and my neck feels stiff."

"Carter?"

"My knee hurts as usual and my lower back aches."

"What about your feelings in a couple of descriptive words, Helen?"

"Oh, tense, worried, maybe even a little scared, but I am hopeful too."

"That's okay. It's possible to have quite contradictory feelings at the same time. How about you, Carter?"

"Definitely skeptical, but willing, and even maybe cautiously curious? Is that a feeling?"

"It sure is," I reply.

For couples who are struggling to make time for homework or whose negative feelings actually make it very hard for them to benefit from homework whether they do it or not, or for couples who want to jumpstart their relationship, I often recommend a weekend intensive. Years ago, I playfully called it Camp Treadway. The name has stuck, but in essence, it's a kind of a couple bootcamp.

The weekend helps couples do a deep immersion in "effortful love" between our sessions while they're on their own, while dealing intensively with some of their hard and stuck issues in the daily sessions with me. The essential idea of the weekend is to help couples learn how to be together, do activities, share feelings, and take turns following and leading without being dependent on or controlled by their own or their partner's feelings.

Most couples tend to feel closest when they are experiencing the same good feelings about anything from the sunset to the dinner or each other. Shared same feelings often are what makes a couple feel connected. What I try to help them experience in this weekend is that they can share feelings even when those feelings are quite different and even difficult, and that can feel intimate, too. They learn that by continuing to do the exercises, their feelings will evolve. That's why I was delighted that despite Carter's initially skeptical attitude, he felt curious. That's a very good sign.

This is the description of the weekend I give couples to consider before they commit to the weekend.

Introduction

The heart of the weekend intensive is helping you be more comfortable with each other's discomforts and differences, to be able to share your feelings without shame or "shoulds," and to hear the other's feelings without taking them too personally. The core goal is for you to learn how to have and share whatever feelings you have without getting caught in them. Just share them and move on to whatever the next activity is on the schedule. It's not about having a good feeling or shared feelings; it's about learning how to feel close and connected with whatever feelings you are having.

The retreat generally begins on a Thursday for a late afternoon session of two hours to plan the time together and set the therapeutic agenda. Then there is a two-hour session on Friday at midday, and Saturday at noon is the two-hour ending session. Then there's a follow-up session once a week for the next three weeks. The follow-up sessions are critical for success in translating the gains of the weekend into your regular life. Keeping the exercises and changes going when you're at home is essential.

Outside of the time with me, the retreat is divided into three blocks per day (morning, afternoon, and evening). You will take turns being the leader of blocks, until the last morning where you will decide together about block activities. Each block will have a least two structured exercises followed by a check-in (to be practiced in our first meeting). In addition to exercises, there will be plenty of time for recreational events on your own. This isn't all work.

However, it is essential that you commit the whole time to focusing on yourselves and the relationship. Please arrange thorough coverage for work and children. Plan on staying in a hotel. And not using electronics except for urgent situations.

Exercise possibilities: Pick two exercises per block from this list, one for the beginning of the block. The block leader is in charge when to do the exercises and the rest of the activities of the block, like recreation and meals, except the follower has to be able to say no if an idea makes them too uncomfortable. Sample exercises:

a) Assigned Mary Oliver poetry readings
b) Trust walk (taking turns leading your partner around for ten minutes with their eyes closed)
c) Trust fall (taking turns falling backward into your partner's arms)
d) Face or hand or foot massage (three minutes each)
e) Hug for thirty seconds
f) Metta (loving kindness) phrases (take turns one of you saying it for both of you)

- *May we be safe and protected*
- *May we have ease of mind and comfort of heart*
- *May we see ourselves with love and compassion*
- *May we be at peace*

g) Walk silently while holding hands for twenty minutes
h) Share favorite or painful childhood memories for fifteen minutes
i) Back massage for fifteen minutes
j) Review ten key ingredients to making a successful relationship (see appendix)
k) Talk and Listen exercise (separated by at least an hour) (see appendix)
l) Tender Loving Care exercise (see appendix)
m) Decision-making protocol (see appendix)
n) Make out for five minutes (Tips appendix)
o) Loving fingers/hurt and angry feelings (Tips appendix)
p) Seduction/rejection role play (Tips appendix)
q) Timed conversational T&L (appendix)
r) Share childhood pictures and stories.

After each exercise, the couple does the brief check-in that Carter and Helen did in my office. Bodily sensations and emotional feelings are named and shared, but not discussed or processed. The couple is encouraged not to discuss their feeling states about the weekend and their relationship except in the formal Talk/Listen exercises or with me when we're meeting. In other words, couples try to learn how to let feelings just be feelings—positive, neutral, or negative—without being judged or debated or turning them into problems to be fixed. This can be a surprisingly liberating experience. Especially when couples' feelings change on their own without either of them having to do anything. It just happens.

Helen started our Friday two-hour session by reporting, "I was surprised to see how much I watched Carter like a hawk. What's going on? Is he okay? Is he mad at me? Does he think this whole thing is a waste of time and money? I mean, I've known that I focus a lot on Carter's moods, but I had no idea how intense it was. There wasn't any room for me at all. Everything was about him. He did say some negative stuff during the check-ins, but he was going along with everything without any complaints. And I was just making up all kinds of bad feelings he was likely having and then feeling upset about stuff that I made up. It was really surprising."

"How about for you, Carter?"

"Well, actually, I liked being able to say negative things and not feel apologetic. I do tiptoe around her a lot because she's always needing reassurance that things are okay. To be honest, I lie a lot. I just say what she wants to hear."

"Dammit, Carter, that sounds really patronizing," Helen said. "You've never said that before."

"I sure have. Maybe you've never listened before," he said sharply.

"Hold on, guys, I want to do something different with these hard feelings that are getting stirred up, is that okay?"

They nodded.

I was actually glad we'd stumbled into this familiar briar patch of theirs. So far, the weekend had been going almost too well.

"So, I would like you to do the check-in right now. Close your eyes and go inside. And when you get to centering on how you're feeling, go ahead and give your feelings a rating on a 0 to 10 scale. Zero being absolutely comfortable relaxed and happy, and 10 being really agitated, angry, sad, uncomfortable.

"Okay. Start with the breaths and then noticing."

They sat quietly and then I asked them gently if they had identified their 0 to10 rating on their feelings. They nodded again.

"Okay guys, this part is going to be a little weird. I want you to just continue to have the feelings you're having, and I am going to step out of the room. When I do, I want you to hug each other without saying a word."

I stepped out for thirty seconds and then gently knocked on the door. They were back on the sofa and smiling a little shyly.

"I wasn't at all sure I wanted him to hug me," Helen said, looking relieved.

"It was surprising given how contrived it was," Carter said. "Wasn't bad, anyway."

"Well, being able to turn toward each other when you feel like turning away is the point of it all. Well done."

In our therapy sessions, Carter and Helen did some deep and hard work around very painful parts of their relationship. But instead of going their separate ways, they were invited to just continue being together even if they were having some difficult feelings. This is the essence of the weekend.

Couples rarely have the time and opportunity to focus on themselves and their relationship in a concentrated way. And to have a prescribed structure with all kinds of activities they have never done before without them having to negotiate it all is freeing. Most important, rarely are couples able to make room for each other's feelings and responses without being reactive and taking them personally. They are invited to be just two people sharing a new adventure without prior history and with being burdened with goals, and at the same time dig in and deal with hard, raw, emotional issues with me. Learning how to open to tough stuff and then collaboratively put it aside to do these funky exercises can be startlingly freeing for couples.

7

THE AMENDS AND FORGIVENESS PROTOCOL

Mary was dressed and coiffed impeccably for this session. Charles wore a tie and coat. They are a very attractive, dignified couple in their late sixties.

Mary held her notes in front of her. I noticed her hands were shaking. She looked around and found the tissue box.

"Are you ready, Mary," I asked gently.

She nodded.

I turned to Charles and said, "I know this will be very hard to hear. You guys have been married for forty years and have done the best that you could, but there has been a lot of hurt and pain caused by each of you regardless of your intentions. I want you to try and hear Mary's pain with fresh ears and a compassionate heart. If you feel yourself shutting down or getting reactive, let me know and we'll take a break, and you and I will step into the next room so I can help you calm down and reconnect. And remember, you too will have a turn. But for now, both of us will do our best to open our hearts to Mary's story. Are you feeling ready?"

"As ready as I'll ever be," he said with a wan smile. I nodded to Mary.

"Okay," she said, and without looking at Charles, she began.

"I am going to begin by talking about something from a long time ago that I've never brought up before. You probably won't even remember.

"You know I was a really good Catholic school girl, and I waited until we got married. But as you also know, I really liked doing 'it' once we started. And we did 'it' all the time. There was one day in the first year we were married when I wanted to surprise you, and so I greeted you at the door when you came home from work wearing only a sexy black negligee, and I had a glass of champagne with two straws in it.

"You looked shocked and tried to make a joke, and said something like, 'What have you been doing, lying around in bed all day, drinking?'

"I was so crushed and ashamed and embarrassed that I poured out the drink, threw out the negligee, and, as you know, have never initiated sex again in our marriage."

Then Mary burst into tears and began sobbing. Charles looked stricken.

"I do, I do remember," he said, and he reached out and took his wife's hand. His eyes filled with tears. "I am so sorry."

Charles and Mary had never talked about this devastating incident, and they had raised three kids and had a pretty decent marriage. But they came in for therapy because they were very distant and remote from each other, and with the kids having left home, they were unsure about the future of their marriage. I had assumed they would choose the behavioral change approach, but Mary was pretty clear from the start she thought they ought to deal with the past. And as it turned out, she was right.

So far we've been focused on couples who choose the Effortful love—behavioral change choice. However, many couples choose in the first session to do the Amends work.

Couples routinely choose the Amends and Forgiveness Protocol as a way of starting therapy when there have been egregious issues like affairs, addictions, and abuse, and I will be discussing those situations later. In this chapter. I want to address the couples who have accumulated profound hurts, and anger, distance, and defenses throughout the history of the marriage from what I call "death by a thousand cuts."

We all do hurt each other in so many small ways in the evolution of our lives as a couple, and we do so over and over again as we try to repair, move on, forgive, and forget. When Mary and Charles were discussing which option to approach to start their therapy, Mary said with deep sadness, "Gee, we've tried and tried, but nothing's worked, and sometimes I feel like there is too much water under the bridge. There are so many issues we've never dealt with, but so many fights are the same old fight. Maybe we do need to deal with the past first before we can get a fresh start."

When Mary took her turn, her list of painful accumulated hurts took her an hour to read, and they covered the full breadth of their forty-one-year marital history. I helped Charles stay open and as compassionate as he could be. At one point in the session when he looked really overwhelmed and began to shut down, we paused and I took Charles out of the room to check on him. He started to cry and said, "I feel like I was a horrible husband." I helped him regain his composure and recognize that by opening his heart to her pain, he was actually being a very good husband.

When one member of a couple hurts the other, obviously they can't take it back. Being able to bear witness to your partner's pain without being defensive when you've caused it is the gift that heals.

The Amends and Forgiveness Protocol is a very formal and choreographed process for helping couples acknowledge, apologize, and forgive each other for all the ways they have been hurtful to each other over the course of the relationship.

Here's the handout I give them that describes the process.

The Amends and Forgiveness Protocol

1) Each member of the couple has as much time as needed to discuss the ways in which they feel hurt, abandoned, betrayed, and disappointed in the relationship, while the therapist and their partner bear compassionate witness. This may take one or more sessions per individual.
2) The listening partner writes an Amends letter that involves directly taking responsibility for having done harm, describing how they hope to insure that they won't repeat the harm, and offering a willingness to negotiate some kind of amends actions they will take.
3) The Amends letter is read in the session, and then the couple negotiates some amends actions. These actions would demonstrate to the hurt partner that not only is their partner saying "I am sorry" in the letter but also is showing they are sorry in a sustained way by their actions. The hurt partner is invited to work on forgiveness,

which is a slow process that doesn't really become possible until their partner has followed through for a sustained period of time with their Amends Actions.

4) The partner who made the amends now goes through the same process described above: they have their own turn to speak their hurts, hear the amends, and try to forgive.

With most couples, one member has been the more vocal complainer/critic and the other has been more silent and shutdown. For purposes of this protocol, letting the vocal one go first almost always works best. It's more comfortable for the couple, and inevitably the more vocal member feels strongly that they have never been truly heard. Many of the sessions are similar to the example of Charles and Mary. It is very difficult to be the "listener" in one of these sessions.

I remember one client couldn't tolerate being on the sofa with her husband while he was going through his hurts. I asked where she might be able to be in the room where she could be most present to him. She chose to stand at the window with her back to him and her hands pressed against the glass. As he continued, she just stood there, shoulders shaking, tears silently running down her cheeks. She really listened.

I help my clients edit their amends letters because often clients have difficulty really taking ownership of their hurtful behavior in a direct way. Frequently clients start sentences with covert defensiveness like, "I am sorry your feelings were hurt when you felt I didn't let you have much of a say-so with the kids," which in some ways isn't acknowledging their own behavior but blaming it on the partner's sensitivities. "I am sorry that I didn't let you have much of a say-so with the kids" is a much stronger sentence.

Here's a copy of Charles's amends letter to Mary. It was relatively short and to the point and a little business-like, but I felt it truly expressed his feelings well and in his way, so I didn't need to edit it at all.

Dear Mary,

I am so sorry about all the ways I hurt you throughout our marriage. Beginning with the first thing you talked about. I am so sorry I shamed you about you trying to be sexy and seductive when we were first married and I am also sorry that I never brought it up or even asked why you didn't initiate sex all these years.

And I really get how much I left it up to you to raise the kids, always in the guise of saying "Mom knows best."

It is true that I put my work first and that it fed my own ego. I am sorry for all the parent conferences, school plays, and sporting events I either showed up late for or didn't make all.

I am sorry that I never stood up for you when my mother critiqued how our house looked and how our children behaved.

I understand how alone you felt when Jonathan had his drug problems in high school and I wouldn't do family counseling.

And it's true that I retreated to watching sports and playing golf rather than really talking or listening to you.

I am also sorry that I was critical of how you spent money when you were basically so careful and managed our whole budget.

There are more items I could review, but these seem to be the main ones. As you said in our session, "I didn't partner with you," and that covers a lot of my failings. I am really sorry for that.

Dearest, Mary, I haven't been the greatest husband, maybe not even a very good one, but I have loved you all these years. Truly. I do hope to make a fresh start. I do want to make amends. I do want our relationship to work.

Love,
Charles

After Charles read the letter to her, Mary looked a little tense and uncomfortable. I stepped in quickly.

"I imagine, Mary, that you're feeling like you should be experiencing a flood of warm, loving feelings in response to Charles's letter, and yet we all know that a few words, no matter how heartfelt, don't make up for forty-one years of feeling lonely and taken for granted."

"That's true, Dr. Treadway, I feel like I should feel more responsive. Mostly I just feel sad."

"Well, this takes time, and that's why the Amends Actions are so key. Charles following through with some action steps can really demonstrate that he means his apology, that he's not forgetting, and that every time he does an Amends Action step, he's sending you a love note of recommitment to you and your marriage. And, Charles, since there's nothing you can do about how you have been all these years, the Amends Actions are key for you too. They will give you things to do that will make you feel better about yourself as a husband and partner, and you will see that this followthrough really matters to Mary. Successful Amends Actions will make it possible for Mary to learn how to truly forgive you and step into building a better relationship with you."

***

Some couples decide to do it differently. They each have a turn first with sharing their feelings and then writing each other the letters, then they follow by negotiating the steps each will take. Charles and Mary agreed that Charles would start some Amends Actions before taking his turn, which was wise because they both felt that Mary was the more injured party.

They came up with two Amends Actions that pleased Mary.

1) For three months, Charles would bring her coffee every morning before leaving for work.
2) Charles initiates going on a long walk with her an hour every weekend at least until the end of the season.

Charles readily agreed to these actions steps, and I emphasized as strongly as I could that the whole effort was dependent on his follow-through in doing these steps. I also stressed that the action steps are a sacred commitment, and that forgetting to do them really could reopen the old wounds we were trying to heal.

For a couple of sessions I monitored Charles's followthrough, which was excellent, and Mary's response, which steadily softened as she realized that Charles was really going to "walk the walk." Then it was Charles's turn.

Charles's sessions were actually less than an hour (by far). His main point to Mary was about how critical and fault-finding she was. He said at one point, "I feel like you never noticed the things I did well and only noticed what I did wrong. You made me feel like I was a failure as a husband and a father. Especially when Johnny was in trouble and you blamed it on me being an 'absentee Dad.' That hurt a lot."

Mary's note of apology was short and direct. She took complete ownership of being constantly critical, judgmental, and complaining. Then at the end of her note, she wrote,

Charley, I loved you so much with all my heart, and I felt you didn't love me that way. It made me so sad and feel so bad about myself that I couldn't stand it. And I couldn't talk about it. Then I just became a nagging bitch. I am so sorry. I think my complaints were my tears (not that I am trying to make an excuse.) It was wrong, and I am so sorry that I tore you down so much of the time.

I do love you, and I am glad we're doing this.

***

Mary cried as she read this to him. And he teared up, too.

So did I.

8

THE CHALLENGES OF INFIDELITY

"It was just a few one night stands, Dr. Treadway. They didn't mean anything, and besides, it's not like anything was going on in our bedroom. Ever since Tara was born, nada."

"Great, Bob, now it's going to be my fault that you picked up women in bars. I can't handle this bullshit," Carol said furiously.

"Hold on you, two. Here's a dilemma for us to consider. If we get into the ongoing difficulties with the marriage as a kind of excuse for lies and betrayal, that often inflames the hurt spouse just in the way Carol is responding. On the other hand, people in Bob's shoes are often desperately unhappy and feeling hopeless in the relationship, and they do justify their own hurtful behavior by blaming their partner. Bob seems to be basically a good guy, and yet he did some really bad stuff: lying to you, Carol, and even putting your safety at risk. But it's not actually surprising (even though completely unfair) that he would utilize his resentment toward you and the relationship to rationalize his behavior.

"Does this make sense?"

"Listen, Dr. Treadway, I can't work with him blaming me for him having random hook-ups, and, when I accused him of it, looking me right in the eye and lying about it. I can't deal with that."

"Well, that's the reason why generally I help couples deal with the acting-out behavior and the lying first before trying to work on repairing and improving the marriage. I would want you, Carol, to feel that Bob really understood how hurtful he's been, took full responsibility for his actions, and was committed to not repeating them. And for you, Bob, by the time we start work on improving this marriage, I want you to feel like you've done everything you can do to make amends so that you can be a full and equal partner to working on the marriage rather than just the designated 'bad guy' in the couple.

"But you two will have to consider whether this approach makes sense. I had one couple who agreed that they didn't want to talk at all about the extramarital stuff and just wanted to work on making the marriage better. And they made that work."

"There's no way something like that would work for us," Bob said ruefully. "I know we've got to deal with the shit I did first."

Infidelity comes in many forms in a marriage. Porn addiction, chat room phone sex, use of prostitutes, love affairs, and even emotional affairs without literally overt sexual behavior can do tremendous harm to a marriage. The betrayal is not so much defined by the behavior but by the deception and secrecy that accompanies it. Even though most people going outside the marriage justify their behavior with complaints about the relationship, it almost always works best for the couple to deal with the affair and betrayal first. I frequently say to couples that the choice to secretly go outside the marriage is 100 percent that partner's fault even though the difficulties in the marriage are both partners responsibility; 50-50. I still want couples to consider their options and choose the course of their therapy, but I do share my bias pretty openly. It is based on decades of experience that the couple has the best chance of recovery if they begin with dealing with the affair.

As with Carol, the person who has been betrayed tends to feel that their life has not only been shattered, but they have been living in a sham world and they were foolish for not guessing something was going. This leads them to want to ask an enormous amount of detailed when, where, what, how, and why questions. Frequently the cheating partner either defensively minimizes or leaves out details, self-protectively lies for fear that the whole truth might destroy the marriage, or literally forgets details. It's often this relentless, out-of-control questioning interaction that sinks the couple's chances of recovery.

Stages of Therapy

Right from the beginning, I provide a treatment plan that has been successful for other couples. Often couples come in amid the crisis of an affair with one or both of them assuming that divorce is inevitable. I want them to know that there is a pathway to recovery, and I want to help them give themselves the gift of time to explore the possibility of reconciliation and healing before making any decisions. I become the holder of the hope.

Step 1: Crisis Management

The first step involves helping the couple work to together to negotiate how to co-exist while giving themselves the time needed to work on the issues. They have a daunting list of issues to work out.

a) They first need to decide whether they should live together, possibly in separate bedrooms, or have a therapeutic separation.
b) They need to have safe ways of talking about the issues in a structured, time-limited fashion. The formal Talk/Listen format (fifteen scheduled minutes of active listening separated by at least twenty-four hours) or the interactive three-minute turns are the only times the partners are encouraged to talk about the details/questions/feelings of the affair(s) outside of my office.
c) Couples have to learn how to effectively use Time-Outs to interrupt escalating out-of-control conflict.
d) They also need to utilize me to vent to, and I encourage them to write me emails or call me between sessions. It is often essential that they each have individual therapy and group support. I also make clear to them that there will be time and place for all the questions that are helpful to ask and answer.

With Bob and Carol, I said, "Couples do get through these shattering events. But you will need the gifts of structure and of time to heal.

There's a plan that will give you guys a fighting chance to recover, but it takes discipline and patience. We will be working on helping you first coexist safely and then carefully manage how to co-parent, deal with what to tells friends and families, and work to keep the lid on all these incredibly painful and provocative feelings except in structured and careful ways at designated times and places."

Step 2: Disclosure

I said to Bob and Carol, "The next step is called the 'Disclosure Process,' which will involve you presenting a timeline of all your transgressions, Bob. Then Carol, you will have the opportunity to ask all your questions. Which can be challenging because questions beget questions. The more you ask, the more you will be trying to understand."

"Yes, Dr. Treadway, he always answers with, 'I forget' or 'It didn't matter.' It just infuriates me. I'm home with our child late into the evening. He's called and said he has to work late. And I am being the stupid, supportive housewife keeping dinner warm on the stove while he's off with prostitutes. What was he thinking? You bet I have questions."

I turned to Bob and said, "You need to understand that's Carol's reality. Her life has been shattered. You may have rationalized this as no big deal. What she didn't know won't hurt her. But now all of a sudden, she's reconstructing her whole last three years around 'What was he doing while we were doing x, y, or z?' It's a nightmare."

"I'm trying to get that," he whispered.

Step 3: Amends and Forgiveness

I said, "Then we will do the Amends and Forgiveness step, which will mean you, Carol, will have an hour or two to say to Bob all your feelings about what he has done. Then Bob will respond with a careful, compassionate letter of taking full responsibility. I will help him do that.

"Then we will discuss what Amends actions he might take to demonstrate the depth and sincerity of his apology. In one case, a woman insisted that her husband sell his share in the family estate on Nantucket where his family had summered for four generations. He had taken his mistresses there for weekend getaways off-season. He was horrified by the request, but in this case it was non-negotiable. In most cases the requests are a little less draconian, but they do need to be truly meaningful.

"I remember another husband who asked his wife, who'd had an affair with her boss, to leave her job, and they ultimately negotiated that she would transfer to a different department. One of the most tender Amends actions I've seen was when a woman asked her husband to give up drinking for a year. This was a guy who was a very infrequent and moderate drinker. Initially he was puzzled by the request, but for that year at every dinner party, holiday celebrations, and family events when he asked the waitress for 'Just water, thanks,' he was communicating directly to her that he was remembering her pain and still expressing his apology. And besides, they now had their own shared secret. It was healing."

It's only after the Amends and Forgiveness project is well underway that the couple considers together how to improve their marriage. But they do so with the knowledge that a history of lies and betrayal casts a very long shadow.

You might have noticed that there's a lot of me talking to Bob and Carol and laying out an extensive set of plans. But knowing that there's a tried-and-true path up this dangerous mountain and that I am an experienced guide often helps folks settle down.

However, my speech is not what's most important; what matters is the conversation they have that follows.

Carol sounded skeptical when she responded. "This all sounds well and good, but I don't think you will follow these rules."

"There you go, just jumping in and judging me. Like you always do."

"But is she right, Bob?" I asked.

"No, dammit!"

I jumped in. "Carol, you have no reason to trust him right now, but let's give him a chance. It could be the first step to real change."

"I will do this if he will."

Step 4: Creating a New Marriage

By the time a couple is ready to start repairing their marriage, they have already incorporated many of the tools of communication and effortful love that are typical of my regular couple therapy. They have already begun the process of change.

Yet it is often very important for both of them to feel like they are truly beginning anew. I remember how much my sons and I couldn't wait to get on the chairlift after a night of a snowstorm. We wanted to be the first ones up for the pure joy of creating fresh tracks in the new powder. Just as we did, couples want (and need) to begin leaving fresh tracks. Couples often do rituals like burning up the journals, letters, and writings of the prior work, or buying something new for the house, or even doing some kind of recommitment ceremony as way of giving themselves a new start—fresh tracks.

Despite their progress, reconnecting with intimacy and sexuality is often the last hurdle. Clearly, sexual intimacy can be re traumatizing for one or both members of the couple because it stirs up images of what happened outside the relationship. I encourage them to wait until this step in their work before even trying to find their way back to each other in the bedroom.

Many of the exercises I discussed earlier around sexuality and intimacy work well because they are new, not part of the past, and they provide structure and slow pacing combined with open communication. Couples who are successful in recovery often feel like they have a new and improved marriage, like the guy I mentioned earlier who said delightedly, "We have a brand-new marriage, and the lawyers didn't get a dime."

However, the shadow of betrayal is long. Even when couples do very well, true trust is the slowest feeling to return.

I told Bob and Carol this story of another couple slowly healing from an affair.

"This couple had done profound, deep work recovering from his long-term affair with his secretary, who she also had known for years. They both gave their all to the effort and had graduated from therapy three years later.

"They came back in two years later to tell me about their painful moment on their vacation to Charleston," I continued. "The wife began by saying, 'We were having a great time window shopping along a street like Newbury Street in Boston, just strolling along holding hands, when he saw a dress in the window and said, 'Look at that, you would look great in it.'

"She paused for a moment and then said, 'I looked at it and instantly knew it was not my kind of dress at all . . . but it was his secretary's style. I turned toward him with tears in my eyes. "Who are you thinking about?" I asked. And you know what, Dr. T., he winced, but he didn't get the slightest bit defensive. His face looked so pained. He took me in his arms and whispered over and over again, 'I'm so sorry. I'm so sorry.'

"The pain was still there for both of them, right below the surface," I went on. "But they could hold the pain together. They could hold each other."

I looked at Carol and Bob. "That was five years after."

Carol and Bob sat silently after listening to the story. Carol reached out her hand and Bob took it.

"Could you ever do anything like that?" she asked

Bob said, quietly, "I don't know, I don't know if I could do that."

"Thanks," said Carol, "That's an answer I can trust."

9

WORKING WITH COUPLES' FAMILY OF ORIGIN ISSUES

Jack's shoulders shook as tears etched his cheeks. His wife, Nancy, was sitting close to him on the sofa. He was holding a photograph of a little boy in a father's arms. The father was in uniform.

"I was only four," he said haltingly, "But I remember this picture. I remember him. This must have been close to the time he went to the war.

"I never saw him again, but I remember. I haven't looked at this picture since I was a kid. Nancy found it. Shit. I wonder what he would think of the mess I've made."

As we seek to find a life partner and make a family, most of us are shaped by our experiences of growing up in our original family. Whether we are looking to replicate our original happiness or avoid our pain or heal our wounds, our childhood relational experiences form the template of our hopes and dreams, our fears, and our defenses that we bring to adult intimate relationships. As Faulkner said, "The past is never dead. It's not even past."

In a significant portion of couples, the learned expectations about what a relationship and family should be like or shouldn't be like are often the triggers that snap couples out of the honeymoon phase and into the "in life" phase of their relationship. When folks are in love, they often experience it as profoundly healing, and their childhood needs and yearnings can feel fulfilled. They are often experiencing the wonderful feeling of being unconditionally loved. But as we know, this phase doesn't last, and the pain and disappointment that ensue often stimulate their old childhood defenses of attacking or withdrawing, trying harder or ignoring, avoiding or seeking soothing elsewhere, and other coping mechanisms.

These psychodynamic issues are familiar to virtually all therapists. Working on this material is often the core of our work with individuals. The extraordinary work of Murray Bowen, Monica McGoldrick, Harville Hendrix, Pia Melody, Sue Johnson, and so many others provide a plethora of models for helping couples understand how their family of origin issues have shaped their relationships. These models are also often highly effective in helping couples be less blaming of each other and more compassionate.

The option of starting with developing a deeper understanding of their family of origin dynamics and how those helped shape the marriage is by far the least chosen of my three alternatives. Even though many partners in my couple therapy are therapists themselves and do frequently prefer the psychodynamic option, they often do so because they've worked on their own family of origin issues and want their spouses to do some of the same. Not surprisingly, their spouses are frequently reluctant to choose this option. Often, they have already felt blamed about their unresolved issues with their family and fear they will get ganged up on in the therapy room.

For clients with very little psychotherapy experience, working on the family of origin seems a little too removed and abstract given whatever their pressing couple needs are. However, I do offer it, and when it becomes apparent in the unfolding work that family of origin issues are playing a salient role in the couple's dynamics, I may encourage them to take a detour back in to those issues in the middle of our current work.

For example, one couple that I treated with the Amends and Forgiveness Protocol seemed to have some glaring family of origin issues going on, and we decided to take a brief detour into having a session about their family dynamics in the midst of doing the amends work.

For couples choosing the family of origin direction either at the beginning of the therapy or later on, I call the first session I do the Pictures session.

I ask each member of the couple to bring in ten to fifteen pictures of themselves and their parents and siblings from their childhoods up through their adolescence. The other member of the couple and I invite the one with the pictures to show us what they chose and explain why, which gives me the opportunity to ask focused questions about their experiences as children.

One or both members of many couples have experienced traumatic childhood. However, even those who have not still carry the pain and disappointments and struggles of even pretty normal childhood lives.

Even though Jim and Cindy didn't have any trauma material, there was plenty to work on. In the Pictures session with them, Cindy's first picture was one of her as an infant pushing away from her mother, who was holding her wearing a tight smile that looked forced.

"This captures Mom and me perfectly. She was holding on too tight, and I obviously wanted to get away."

And then there was a school picture of Cindy in third grade. She was in a white communion dress, and her blonde hair was parted in the middle and pulled tightly into perfectly braided pigtails. She stared blankly at the camera with a polished, professional smile.

"What does this one mean to you?" I asked.

"I call that 'the look,'" she said with a little bit of pride. "A lot of my pictures look like that: a pretty little dressed-up 'good girl,' always smiling. To be honest, I sort of hid behind that smile. So nobody could get to me."

Next she showed us a family photo of her mom and dad and her two older brothers; the whole family seemed to have glazed smiles on their faces.

"What do you see here," I asked.

Cindy suppressed a chuckle and said, "Well, it looks like I'm not the only one hiding behind a smile."

Jim chimed in. "You should see them on the holidays. They all look like this picture all the time. That's why I call being with them FFF, which is short for 'Forced Family Fun.'"

They both laughed. But Jim laughed much harder.

"And how does this show up between the two of you in your marriage?" I asked.

"Well, let me tell you—"

"Wait a second, Jim, before you launch, how about you answer that question first, Cindy."

"He's always bringing up what phonies they are, and it's true, but then he's complaining all the time that I'm not being 'real' with him and he doesn't know how I really feel about him."

Jim jumped in. "But that's because you always—"

"Hold on," I interrupt Jim for the second time. "It's important that we stay focused on Cindy's experience here. In a few minutes, we'll be looking at your pictures and perhaps understanding your back story a little better, too."

When we did get to Jim's pictures, we saw him looking like a fierce and strong boy who tended to glower at the camera. His younger brother and sisters, four in all, seemed much more relaxed and comfortable.

"So, what do you make of yourself in this picture, Jim? You seem sterner than your siblings."

"Well, that's around the time my dad completely checked out. I found out later that he was having an affair instead of 'working late,' which was always the story. I don't know how old I am in this picture, maybe nine, but that's when my mom kind of put me in charge of my little brothers and sisters. She was checked out, too. I didn't realize back then she was already beginning to drink a lot. Lot of secrets in my house. I suppose I do look mad, but I don't remember feeling like that at the time. I kinda liked being in charge and my mom depending on me a little. It made me feel important."

"So it sounds like there was an empowering side of being the oldest, and yet there was a lot of hidden stuff going on," I said, moving to the obvious connection to his sensitivity about Cindy's "hiding behind her smile."

"You know, Jim and Cindy," I said as I sat back in my chair and addressed them both. "There's a way in which pictures don't lie, and yet this whole deal can sound a little glib, so bear with me. I do have a sense, Cindy, that your reticence and tendency to hold back feels to Jim like you're holding back or hiding something. And Jim, you're frustration and tension may show up more as anger for Cindy, who was always trying to be the 'good girl' and protect herself."

Jim laughed and said, "You're right, that does sound pretty glib."

At the end of the session, I said, "So each of you pick the picture you like the most of yourself, the one that best captures what it felt like to be you, and exchange them. What I would like you to do, Cindy, is from time to time in the upcoming weeks, pause and look with compassion at Jim's picture. Really look at that tense little boy from long ago who was probably carrying the weight of the world on his shoulders. And Jim, I want you look at this picture of the perfectly presented little girl, and remember the first one we saw of the baby pushing away from her mother and clearly crying. Try to hold with tenderness that little girl who was trained to smile.

"There's more to talk about here."

When Trauma Is Involved

Frequently family of origin explorations reveal that one or both members of the couple have experienced significant trauma, such as physical or sexual abuse or abandonment and neglect. Many couple therapists tend to refer the client out for individual therapy when those issues arise. However, I see helping one or both members of a couple deal with their childhood trauma issues as a profound opportunity to help couples feel more deeply connected and close. Often both individual work and bringing the issues into the couple therapy works best. Having your partner (not just the therapist) be present as you open to your childhood pain can be a source of profound comfort and healing.

Every childhood has struggle, pain, and insecurity. When working with couples in which one member has a significant trauma history and the other had a pretty normal childhood, it is still important to focus on the spouse who had an easier time growing up and engage with the pain of their struggles as well. It is essential that the spouse with the trauma history not feel like they are suddenly turned into the "identified patient."

When one or both members of the couple have had significant trauma, it is useful to work directly on those issues. We will have a few sessions utilizing what I call conjoint individual work; we divide the sessions in half, and I focus on each member of the couple in the presence of the other. When one member of the couple is in the non-participatory listening role, they often become less defensive and more compassionate to their partners as their partners deal with their childhood pain (as in the picture session). And we may divide the time differently if one member of the couple clearly has the more significant trauma history, and the focus may be more on how the partner can be positively supportive of the trauma survivor.

Therapy Goals

There are three key goals for working well with individual members of the couple who have trauma histories in their families of origin.

1) Deepen their understanding of what happened growing up in their family so that they can better understand the impact of their childhood on their relationships in the present.
2) Empower them to take charge of conducting their relationships with their abusive parent rather than remaining trapped in a helpless, reactive, one-down position.
3) Help them work through their grief and recognize that their childhood hurts were not their fault, forgive themselves for learning maladaptive coping behaviors in their childhood, and change those behaviors in their adult lives.

Nobody escapes childhood unscathed, but children growing up in an abusive family system bear heavier scars than most. The very survival strategies that helped them manage the chaos of growing up often become major impediments to successfully engaging in adult relationships.

Childhood Coping Skills in Adult Relationships

Most trauma survivors are unaware of the relationship between their early life experiences growing up in a dysfunctional family and the problems that bring them into treatment. Yet due to the legacy of low self esteem, difficulties with trust, unresolved dependency, and blocked affect, trauma survivors are likely to develop a wide variety of maladaptive coping styles. A strong fear of being hurt and an equally strong need for nurturance are usually the prime motivating forces for survivors in their adult relationships. For most survivors, these needs for safety and intimacy are mutually exclusive. Intimacy is based on the partners being trusting, affectively available, and interdependent. For survivors this is a very unsafe position, one that almost always evokes the sense of danger, dread, and entrapment from childhood.

Thus, survivors often struggle unconsciously to find a form of intimacy that doesn't sacrifice safety. Many survivors simply avoid becoming too close to others, preferring a life alone to the risks of being hurt in a close relationship. Others find ways to engage in self-protective partial intimacy. They may find emotional closeness acceptable but sexual intimacy impossible, or vice versa. They may become emotional pursuers, thereby avoiding the anxiety of waiting to be sought after. Alternately, they may play the role of distancer, avoiding the risk of rejection. Some individuals manage by maintaining multiple relationships rather than putting all their emotional eggs in one basket.

Finally, in their adult relationships survivors tend to seek emotional reparations for the hurts of childhood, which almost always fails. No matter how much the spouse loves the survivor, he/she can't really make up for the past and will often feel inadequate. Spouses become frustrated and tend to distance themselves because they feel that nothing they do is ever good enough. This response only confirms the survivor's worst fear, which is that other people will ultimately hurt them or abandon them.

Denise was a very successful woman in her middle thirties who ran a business and a household in an extremely competent way. However, she and her husband, Rob, disagreed strongly about having children, and they came to therapy about that. Her position was that children were too demanding and would wreck her career and maybe her marriage. Denise and Rob fought about becoming parents as well as about her controlling behavior and her inability to let him take the lead in any area in their lives. Denise knew that her behavior was getting in the way of her marriage, and she knew that her resistance to having children was probably somehow rooted in her childhood. She had learned to manage very competently living with a severely alcoholic mother after her dad left when she was five.

I remember a session in which she was explaining her childhood morning routine to her husband and me. Her mother would be passed-out drunk, usually on the living room sofa, and Denise would get herself dressed for school, get her little brother dressed, make breakfast and pack lunches, and then take her brother by the hand and walk to their school bus.

"How old were you, Denise?" I asked gently.

"Oh, maybe, six or seven," she said brightly, as if it was the most normal thing in the world. She was clearly quite proud of her competence.

At the end of the session, I said to her, "So Denise, I'd like you to try something entirely odd, and I would like you to try it without me explaining why. Are you game?"

"You know I don't do games, Dr. T," she said with a teasing chuckle.

"Right, Denise, but I do want you and your husband to do something that may be a little startling for you. May I take him out in the hall and give him a suggestion privately?"

"I don't like surprises, but if you think it will help, I'll do it."

Out in the hall, I told Rob to go to a children's clothing store and have the sales clerk pick out a regular size dress for a six-and-a-half-year-old girl. He looked at me like I had two heads.

In the next session, I said to Denise, "Are you ready? Rob's going to show you something he bought."

Rob put a box in her lap, and she pulled out a little navy-blue polka dot dress and held it up. She turned toward me and said, "It's a little girl dress. What's your point, Dr T?"

"So what age little girl would this dress be for, Denise?"

"I don't know, maybe three or four. It's really small."

"And that is the point. This dress is for a normal size six-and-a-half-year-old girl. Just the age you were when you were getting breakfast and lunches ready and you and your brother off to the bus all by yourself."

Denise teared up, and said, choking, "But it's so small. It's way too small."

And then she started to truly grasp that her fear of having children was really based on how overwhelmed and responsible she felt being a little girl mothering herself and her little brother. She began to understand better why she needed to feel in control much of the time. That was how she had courageously survived and even thrived as a girl.

This type of dramatic breakthrough doesn't happen often, but it does exemplify how childhood coping skills that often worked well can be problematic in adult relationships.

The second step is that I help clients change their relationship to their abusive parent in the here and now. This often means a variety of possibilities like standing up to them differently, working on forgiving them, or more completely disengaging from them. The key is finding the right step for that particular client.

With Marsha, the next right step was learning how to "let go of the rope" in her endless tug-of-war with her abusive mother. Even though her mother was in her eighties, she still criticized and belittled everything about Marsha. Marsha would always react defensively and argue back like a defiant adolescent, and it would make their annual visit enormously stressful and frustrating. In my work with Marsha and her husband, Paul, we agreed to "let go of the rope" by turning her mother's relentless criticism into a private game. They picked seven or eight things to leave awry in the house, like a noticeably crooked painting, clothes draped on a chair in the living room, milk left out on the counter, a disheveled bathroom, a messy desk, or mismatched outfits. And then they each bet how many of the items Marsha's mother would critique and how long it would take her. They also bet on how many other criticisms her mother would make in the course of the weekend. They decided that Marsha would immediately agree with her mother's feedback and fix whatever was pointed out.

Throughout the weekend, the mother pointed out all of the planted imperfections and considerably more, and Marsha remained steadfastly and pleasantly responsive to all of her mother's comments. She also won the bet by anticipating correctly that her mother would find way more things to correct than just what they planned for.

Her mother went away declaring it was the best visit ever and asked Marsha on the way to the airport if she was taking medication. Marsha recognized at a much deeper level that her sense of being a competent, mature woman didn't depend on winning her mother's approval or even fighting back with her mother. And she and Paul thoroughly enjoyed the intimacy of being a playful, conspiratorial team.

The last part of the family of origin work involves addressing the complicated and mixed feelings clients have about themselves as children growing up in dysfunctional or alcoholic families. It always surprises me how much trauma survivors blame themselves for the abuse they experience as children. But young children have no way of understanding that their parents aren't normal, so if a parent is abusive, or drunk, or just completely neglectful, the child thinks that whatever is going is somehow their fault. Helping trauma survivors develop self-compassion instead of self-pity, practice self-care instead of self-indulgence, and become empowered rather than entitled is the core of the healing journey. They can't change the past, but they can learn how not to be prisoners of the past. Survivors learn to accept that even though the defenses they developed as children have often turned out to be self-defeating in adult life, they were useful at the time. An emotionally deprived six-year-old might nurture herself with too much food, an abused boy might become a bully, and a scared eight-year-old might become painstakingly shy. After all, they were just kids.

Sometimes I ask clients to conjure up a mental picture of themselves as children under the age of twelve and imagine what they felt like, what their fears were, how hard they tried, how alone they felt. Then I ask them to consider just for a moment what they would like to give to that child if they could go back in time. These are some of their responses:

"I would tell her that it wasn't going to last forever."
"I would be his friend, and we could play together."
"That it's okay she doesn't know how to make it better."
"A place she could go where she would be safe."
"Just a hug. That would be good enough."
"I would promise him that I will always love him."

There are a variety of ways to help clients nurture themselves more effectively. I encourage clients to develop some healthy self-care like yoga, meditation, and daily exercise, practice affirmations, accept their personality flaws, and learn how to grieve for their lost childhoods. For example, I have one client who never expressed any of her feelings as a child and who survived by hiding behind a wall of silence. She's currently keeping a daily journal in which she takes herself back into childhood feelings and then writes them down. She brings the journal into sessions and reads it. Slowly she's learning to let the little girl she used to be say the things that never got said and be with someone who will gently listen to her.

Survivors bring themselves up the best that they can. Essentially I am teaching my clients how to be their own parent more effectively and lovingly. As they separate their sense of an emerging adult self from the child they once were, they begin to feel more capable of taking risks. The key is recognizing that it is not up to their partner to take care of them and make life safe for them. This is something they do for themselves.

Finally, since almost all of us are stuck in a variety of unresolved relationships with others living and dead, I encourage clients to start a grief book. I tell them to get a big notebook with plenty of blank pages and letters to the people they have difficult, unresolved relationships with, like mothers and fathers and siblings and their own spouse and children and even former spouses, friends, and other people of importance in their lives. Often, one member of the couple will really like this idea and the other be completely uninterested . . . and it is not always dependent on which person had the more traumatic childhood.

The client starts each day by taking a few breaths and then choosing someone to write to in that particular moment. They write a few lines and then go about their day. This process over a couple of months of daily entries allows us to tease out the myriad complex feelings they often have in their most difficult relationships. It allows the client to feel their feelings, externalize them, and begin to let them go. Here are excerpts of entries that a client wrote to her dead, abusive, alcoholic parent.

> 8/13/09
> Dear Dad, (that sounds too personal)
> I've never once written you a letter. It sounds almost artificially close and affectionate to write 'dear.' You were always on one side and us on the other. You made it that way. Your anger and your hostility leaked out of every word, out of every pore, out of every breath, and you weren't even aware of it. I remember being incredulous at your hurt that no one liked you.

8/18/09
I remember being a little girl in church and you standing next to me and seeing your big hand finding the right page in my prayer book. Remembering that "normal" moment makes me so sad.

9/10/09
I remember once when it was just you and me one night at home and you made french fries from scratch. I can remember wanting you to connect with me so badly and it was like I was there making and eating french fries with a stranger. We had nothing to say to each other.

9/15/09
I was afraid of you. I used to sleep in that bottom bunk with three large dolls all around me, two on one side, one on the other, pressing in on me so I only had enough space to be straight in the bed. And I used to pile blankets on the bed no matter how hot it was. It was what I needed to feel safe. I never felt safe. There was nothing I could count on [because] you were so unpredictable. I used to lay in bed and pray to some unknown God, pleading for the faintest glimmer of hope that there could be some change . . .

10/10/09
I'm afraid to start writing again. It has taken me a week to get back to this. I'm afraid of the pain that goes with these words. I've started remembering more and more of my childhood, something I generally split off from and don't remember before the age of 17. I've started to see how much I am today was founded on who I was then.

10/21/09
In my bedroom is a wastebasket lined with a brown paper bag. That bag has your writing on it: "Cupcake." That's what you called me. It was when I was sick and living in my apartment alone. I hadn't been over to the house for a couple of weeks and you brought me some of Ma's homemade chicken soup. That bag, that handwriting, was the last contact I had with you before you died. You're dead. I'm writing a letter to a dead person. You, my father, you're dead. I can't

> throw the bag out. The papers go in, I empty them out, more papers go in, but the bag stays.
>
> 11/21/09
> I still miss the dad I never had.

I believe deeply in the saying, "Grieving alone lasts forever; grieving together heals." Anna read these excerpts to Andrew and me. As she wept frequently throughout, he sat on the sofa with his arm around her, and I listened attentively leaning forward in my chair. In those moments, the girl from long ago was not alone.

10

DIVORCE

The Sword of Damocles

"You mean we have to decide whether we're going to sleep around, Dr. Treadway? I never thought we would come to this," said Carl with tears in his eyes.

"Unfortunately, we do. In order for this therapeutic separation plan to work well, we do need to have some transparency and collaboration around this painful question," I explained. "For some couples, opening up the relationship to possible outside engagements is too risky, and for other couples, insisting on continuing monogamy is much too constraining and undermines the whole point of the separation in the first place.

"Often couples settle on a 'Don't ask—don't tell' policy, with the understanding that if an outside dalliance becomes emotionally serious then the other partner will be told. But there's no one-size-fits-all answer here. We need to find out what's right for the two of you. Why don't you take some time right now answer to talk about it."

For most of human history, divorce was not an option. Bound by religious beliefs and community as well as family and cultural norms, couples stayed together "for better or worse." Nowadays, many of the couples daring marriage come from divorced parents themselves, and they enter it with the knowledge that divorce is a common option for a lot of people and that almost 50 percent of couples get divorced This means that the threat of possible divorce and the confusion over what is a "good enough" marriage permeates couples' lives.

Couples like Jennifer and Carl come into therapy questioning the viability of their marriage. To work well with couples like these, we need to be able to help them go through a safe and potentially positive discernment process to evaluate the pros and cons of staying together versus divorcing. I often say to couples that living in the question of whether to go or stay is much like drinking battery acid; it corrodes the relationship terribly to be always questioning whether it should continue.

Dr. Bill Doherty's work in this area is called Discernment counselling and I would strongly recommend it for further understanding.

Here are some of the alternative options that I offer to couples. And as in the rest of my collaborative couple therapy, I believe that what they carefully choose is likely to work best for them.

Trial Marriage

I invite couples to consider working hard on the relationship in a time-limited fashion (usually up to six months) and wait until then to decide whether enough progress has been made to warrant staying together. I help them work on the relationship without denying their ambivalence about staying in the relationship. I frequently remind couples, those with children in particular, "You still have to work together as parents regardless of whether you're a couple or not. Working well on what might be your last try may help you get a reasonable, non-conflictual divorce that turn makes co-parenting much easier."

Jennifer had announced to Carl that's she was pretty sure she wanted a divorce but was willing to give the marriage a last try because of their three young children. They did the Amends and Forgiveness protocol and worked on communications and behavioral changes. What enabled Jennifer to fully participate in this effort was that she knew how much this effort to give it "one last try" meant to her husband. She hoped that if they did divorce, it would be a less destructive process and they would have a better chance at being a good team as co-parents.

Therapeutic Separation

Despite a good faith effort on both of their parts, Jennifer decided she wanted a therapeutic separation. This is a carefully negotiated process that allows couples to collaborate in taking time apart—while living either in the same house or in separate places. I help couples go through a Therapeutic Separation Protocol that prevents them from doing even more harm to each other during a highly vulnerable time and increases the chances of a "good" reconciliation or a "good" divorce.

Couples have to collaboratively negotiate the difficult issues that need to be addressed to have an effective and constructive separation. Most couples assume that a separation is just an indirect start down the road to divorce. However, sometimes separating may be the key helping couples work together differently and more positively while interrupting their habitual, self-defeating couple behavior. Absence often does make the heart grow fonder. Experiencing that the grass isn't necessarily greener helps folks get perspective, too.

When couples are debating this issue, I will often disclose that my wife and I had a separation in our early years of marriage and it saved our relationship.

Here are the steps that have to be negotiated:

Therapeutic Separation Protocol

1) In the family house or in separate homes.

   Although it often works best for couples to be completely separate for a while, sometimes when there are children or limited finances involved it's best for couples to stay in the same house together, but in separate bedrooms. The understanding is that they will not be trying to be a couple but will work together to be good co-parents and housemates while really stepping away from working on the relationship.

2) Length of time.

   It's hard to decide how long a separation should be. In my experience, three to six months usually works best. Less time tends to have less emotional impact and a longer time tends to increase the possibility of each member moving on with their lives and giving up their marriage as time passes. Usually we initially set a length of time with the agreement that we will reconvene to reconsider the options at a designated time.

3) Co-parenting and visitation with children.

   Couples obviously need to prioritize protecting the kids and providing as much consistence and care as co-parents as they can. I will often have couples bring the kids into therapy to explain what they are doing and how it will work. Kids do best when the adults seem to be working together and are maintaining the kids' lives and routines as stably and as predictably as possible. It's also important when couples are going to be in separate living quarters that, when possible, the parents move back and forth rather than the kids. Kids do best staying in their own home.

4) Finances and legal advice.

   It's essential that couples negotiate finances openly and fairly. I also encourage couples to get a legal consultation about the separation so as to make sure that whatever agreements they make during the separation cannot be used against them in a potential divorce.

5) What to tell children, family, and friends.

   How couples share with others about their marriage and separation others often makes a bad situation worse. Well-meaning family and friends may take sides as a way of trying to be supportive. I encourage couples to come up with an agreed-upon message that puts a positive spin on the situation, like, "We've been working on our marriage and have decided to separate as a way of breaking some of our old, difficult patterns and giving us some time to create new ones. We're hopeful that this might give our marriage a fresh start." Obviously, the situation may be more dire than that sounds, but the couple's marriage is a private enterprise, and I encourage couples not to be too open with others. The exception to this recommendation is that each member of the couple should be able to have one or two friends or family as true confidants, with whom they can share fully. Couples are encouraged to be clear with each other about who their confidants are.

6) Choosing between monogamy or open marriage.

   It is critically important that couples collaboratively negotiate their guidelines around fidelity issues. Couples split between continuing with monogamy because the introduction of outside relationships feels like too much risk to them and doing some version of open marriage, which for some couples is a central element in really being free of the marital bonds. The key here is for couples to collaborate on a shared plan and then keep to it.

7) Continuation of couple therapy during separation.

   When my wife and I separated for six months forty-five years ago, we chose to stay in couple therapy as well as to have one-on-one sessions with our couple therapist. The ongoing connection was essential for us to have a safe way of staying connected, and I don't think our story would have worked out without it. Obviously, our success doesn't make it right for everyone, but most of the couples with whom I do therapeutic separations stay in at least some ongoing therapy with me.

8) Contact with each other, and with the kids.

   In most cases, I recommend that initially couples take as much of a break from each other as possible. If the separation is going to be powerful, couples really need to disengage well for a stretch. This approach is clearly influenced by the age of the kids. With young kids, couples do need to have ways of preserving the kids' sense of family while the parents are apart. Often couples choose to have a family night once a week, even though the parents are being as separate as possible.

   After a couple of months, if the couple is feeling ready to explore more contact, they may experiment with "date" nights or doing some of communications exercises and engagements that they may not have been very successful during earlier phases of treatment.

9) Trial reconciliation.

   Rather than thinking couples are ready for recommitment after a time apart, even if things have gone well, I encourage

> couples to give reconciliation a try before recommitting. They need to experience substantial change and progress while living together before being sure that they should stay married. Making it okay for them to still have some doubts and ambivalence actually takes pressure off and gives them a better chance at success.

When the time came to consider a Trial Reconciliation, Jennifer acknowledged that she was ready to start the divorce process. Neither Carl or I were shocked. Jennifer had been pretty transparent throughout our efforts that she was working on the marriage more for the kids than for herself.

They had been at our couple therapy for a year, and I asked them if it had been worth it since they were ending up in divorce anyway. I was really glad to hear that Carl felt grateful for the effort and accepting of Jennifer's need to end the effort. Jennifer felt she reassured herself that she tried really hard (which she did) and one day she would be able to look her kids in the eyes and say, "I did my best."

We continued through the divorce process doing occasional sessions, particularly around co-parenting issues. They explored the mediation process and collaborative law (where the lawyers work together to protect the rights of each member of the couple while helping them not become adversarial in the process.)

They chose a great collaborative law team and ended up with a good, friendly relationship and became a good co-parenting team. I saw them both individually one last time after the divorce was final.

Carl was actually feeling quite good about having gone through the divorce and had moved on to a new relationship with a woman who really loved him. In my last session with Jennifer, she was very wistful.

"You know Dr. Treadway, it wasn't a bad marriage, and we made a good family together. I just didn't want to be intimate with him that way. But being a fifty-two-year-old single woman isn't exactly a piece of cake."

"Well, it's not like you didn't try really hard. I was there. You worked hard to make it work. I hope the separation gave you enough of a taste of what you would be getting into."

"Yes, I thought I was prepared, but . . ." she paused and then said with some determination, "It will be okay. I chose it."

As she left, I felt a wave of sadness come over me. Yes, she chose divorce, but maybe it was a mistake. Maybe she would come to really regret it. And I couldn't help but wonder what I might have done differently, better.

I have had couples choose to stay together and one or both of them regretted it, and couples choose to get divorced and one or both of them regretted it. How little we actually know about what's right for others, and how little we can be sure that our best efforts are actually what's best for any given couple sometimes haunts me.

11

WHEN ONE SPOUSE IS THE "PROBLEM"

John was a heavyset man with a flushed face that seemed to be in a natural scowl, and Amy was a petite, immaculately coiffed woman with a tight smile and anxious, darting eyes. They sat at either end of my sofa, clearly tense and uncomfortable. After some initial joining, I asked what brought them in.

John jumped in and said, "Well, she'll tell you I have a drinking problem, and that's why we're here."

"Sounds like you don't necessarily agree, John."

"Well, I know I drink more than I should, but I don't know that cutting down or quitting is going to improve everything else in our relationship, like what isn't happening in our bedroom, if you know what I mean."

"Oh, John, why are you bringing that up?" Amy whispered while tearing up.

"Hold on, you two. It sounds like you agreed to come in to address your difficulties around John's drinking, but it seems like there are a whole lot of other difficult issues going on."

"You got that straight!" John said emphatically.

"Well, let's work together on whether we should open up the whole can of worms or start with the issues around drinking and get that sorted out first. Perhaps the two of you can be an effective team around how you guys deal with drinking. Amy can work on her way of responding to the drinking better and with more care. And you can define your own guidelines, John, to managing your own drinking choices. Perhaps each of you can take responsibility for your part in the problem, and that might help the two of you get stronger and be more able to deal with other issues in the relationship. Why don't the two of you talk it through. I'll help you take turns and make sure you're understanding each other's positions well."

"If you can get her to stop nagging me, Doc, that would be a start."

After a ten-minute back and forth with me just coaching them about taking turns and not interrupting each other or dwelling on the past, they ended up agreeing to start with the drinking issue as long as Amy agreed to work on intimacy issues later.

In the first nine chapters of this book, we addressed how to work with couples when the relationship is the overt, explicit presenting problem. However, whether it's substance abuse, process addictions, physical abuse, or mental illness, some couples will begin therapy with one spouse—not the relationship—being the "identified patient" or the "presenting problem". For example, with John and Amy, they had agreed to come in to talk about his drinking issues and what to do about them. Although there are usually complicated relational dynamics at play in addition to the individual issues, it actually may feel safer and more stable emotionally for the couple to be focused on one member of the couple rather than the relationship itself.

Even though couples have come in because of one person being defined as "the issue," sometimes there's a lot of covert or overt disagreement about whether the relationship or the "identified patient" is the problem; this was obviously the case with John and Amy. To create a collaborative therapy, I start by helping couples negotiate whether to prioritize focusing on the presenting problem or the relationship as a whole. Usually couples themselves agree that they need to work on the presenting problem that they walked in with, but it is often a comfort to the identified patient to be reassured that he or she isn't the only problem and that their relational work will be addressed, too. If couples can't agree and they solicit my opinion, I tilt in favor of working with the couple on the presenting problem first because that is the issue that caused them to risk seeking outside professional help in the first place. Relationship changes can begin while being organized around what brought them to therapy in the first place. When couples make progress working as a team on dealing with the presenting problem, it strengthens them to then address the deeper and more vulnerable issues that divide them.

Substance Abuse

Substance abuse is an issue when an individual has a pattern of being dependent on the use of substances (like alcohol and prescribed or illegal drugs to alter or control mood states), when the substance use has a negative impact on sleep and other health issues, or causes hangovers, irritability, or communication issues, as well as a significant negative impact on the user's spouse or others surrounding the user.

Clearly this description is very inclusive. I think substance abuse can and does exist long before anyone sees obvious loss of control or the onset of overt physical, psychological, or interpersonal symptoms such as addiction. My client John thoroughly enjoyed eight to ten beers every night. In his mind, he was always a jovial, mellow drinker. However, he had sleep apnea, was overweight, had erectile dysfunction, often passed out in front of the TV, and had a very unhappy wife. Amy became stronger as the first session went along, and at one point said, "Your beers are your mistress. After your visit with 'her,' the kids and I might as well be the wallpaper!" Even though they came in to therapy to discuss his drinking, John did not think he had a problem. He was only in my office to placate his wife.

When couples are tangled in a battle about one member's individual choices, both members of the couple tend to feel disempowered and helpless because they are focused on their partner changing. Yet in most substance abuse cases, the blame game between the spouses tends to contribute to maintaining the status quo. The essence of working well with couples presenting this way is to get each member of the couple to not point the finger of blame at each other, but to turn that finger toward themselves and change their own behavior.

I call disentangling couples from the blame game around the substance abuse behavior the "Disengagement Phase." I help couples shift from the repetitive argument of "If only you would drink less, then

I would be nicer," and the other saying, "Well, I would drink less if you didn't nag so much." It is empowering for each member of the couple to work on their own actions which they have control over rather than being dependent on the other one changing.

The Disengagement Phase

The disengagement phase emphasizes that the drinker considers options like a controlled drinking contract, a substance abuse consultation, a period of abstinence, observational drinking (in which they keep track of how they feel and respond to each drink), and even considering going to an Alcoholics Anonymous (AA) meeting.

At the same time, I work with their partner to stop how they are engaging around their partner's substance abuse. I make the assumption that whether the partner is criticizing, ignoring, distancing, or pleading, whatever they are doing is likely to contribute to sustaining the substance abuse behavior rather than effectively helping to change it. In other words, if nagging, stop nagging; if shutting down, speak up; if isolated in silence, reach out to friends, individual therapy, even Alcoholics Anonymous.

Later in the session with John and Amy, I said to her, "It sounds like what you characteristically do when John's had a lot to drink is get frustrated with him and often become critical. Is that right?"

Amy looked down and wrung her hands. "That's right, Dr. Treadway, and it doesn't do any good at all."

"Well, I am going to encourage you to take a break from making any comment at all on his drinking, and instead, I would like you to write out all your concerns, fears, worries, and disappointments about the impact John's drinking is having on him, and on you and the kids. Then I would like you to bring it in to read here in the next session. And in the meantime, don't say a peep about it. Does this make sense?"

"Anything is better than fighting about it every night."

"Okay with you, John? It might be a hard letter to hear."

"I am sure I've heard it all before."

"I am sure you have too, John, but that's when she's just ragging on you. I am hoping that in here you will be able to listen a little better. And listening well doesn't mean you have to agree with her," I said with a friendly smile.

The Crisis of Change

Therapy starts with each person changing their own actions. Often what emerges is that the substance abuser is unable to be successful at moderate and controlled use no matter what they commit to in therapy or whatever changes the spouse makes. This often leads to a crisis in the couple relationship.

In John's case, he agreed to drink no more than six beers a day, use a breathalyzer test before driving, and get an alcohol consultation. He was unable to follow through with any of those commitments, which led to me helping the couple work together collaboratively to decide between a therapeutic separation or a classic alcoholism intervention. John was really against separating and chose submitting to an intervention.

The intervention involved his parents, his two sisters, his best friend, Joe, Amy, and the couple's two teenage daughters, Lisbet, fifteen, and Annie, thirteen. Annie said through her tears, "I want the daddy I used to have. All my friends thought you were the best dad, and now I don't ever have them over to the house anymore. I used to be so proud of you, and now I am ashamed."

Nothing Amy could have said could have reached John the way his daughter did in that moment. John went into detox, started AA, and today remains sober. It's been a year, and now John and Amy are making their first tentative steps toward working on their intimate life.

Process Addictions

Whether it's a pornography, sex, video gaming, gambling, spending, hoarding, or eating disorders, process addictions are very similar to substance abuse. They are activities that negatively impact both the addict and their partner, and are difficult to self-regulate in a moderate and balanced manner. If a process addiction is the reason the couple is coming to therapy, it makes sense to begin with treating the problem before the relational issues.

Each member of the couple is encouraged to stop trying to change their partner and take responsibility for their own behavior. If one or both members of the couple are unable or unwilling to keep their commitment to change their own behavior, then I can work with their individual stuckness, their fear of change, and the ways in which the system remaining the same works for them. As with substance abuse, if there is no progress, then ultimately the viability and continuation of the relationship and/or the therapy is called into question.

When Both Members of the Couple Have a Process Addiction

When one member of the couple has a process addiction, couple therapy looks a lot like the work I demonstrated with John and Amy. The couple learns how to be a collaborative team with both members "doing their job" around how they handle the presenting problem.

However, in the case of Alex and Beth, they both agreed right in the first interview that each of them had addictive problems that were getting in the way of their relationship. He acknowledged he spent much too much time gambling online and lost a lot of money, and Beth acknowledged that her excessive diet and exercise routines bordered on anorexia. They had both been in long-term, individual therapies without much success, and they were hoping that somehow working in couple therapy might be effective.

I offered them the choice of working on their couple relationship or learning how to support and partner each other around dealing with their difficult process addictions: his gambling and her dieting.

They were immediately intrigued with the idea of working on how to support each other around their individual issues because they tended to be spending a lot of time being very critical of each other's compulsive behaviors. They also felt very alone in the relationship as they each tried to deal with their individual struggles.

We began doing what I call conjoint individual sessions, in which I work with each of them for twenty-five minutes around their individual issues while in the presence of each other. The witnessing partner is encouraged to open their hearts without having to do anything but listen with as much compassion and empathy as they can while their partner talks with me about their issue.

I use therapeutic structure and guidelines a lot to create safety for couples, but sometimes I shift gears to capture the moment. For example, while Beth and I were working yesterday, she said, "I know I'm not really old. I am only forty-three, but I feel like a dried-up old hag no man would be interested in. I look at pictures of myself in a bikini when I was seventeen and wonder where she went. And it doesn't matter how much weight I lose, I still have ugly stretch marks, and everything sags."

I glanced at Alex, and he had tears in his eyes. Even though it wasn't his turn, I decided to bend the rules and ask him how he was feeling.

He reached for his wife's hand and said, "This man is still very interested in you, sweetie."

And she took his hand.

I think I guessed right by shifting gears. Alex's comment really touched Beth. We will see next session if there was a backlash. Just because an intervention feels good in the moment doesn't mean it is good. I often remind myself of that with the phrase, "More will be revealed."

Physical Abuse

There is one couple situation in which I set firm ground rules and don't risk letting couples decide on the course of therapy. When there is a history of physical abuse or the real possibility of physical abuse in a couple system, it is essential to establish a contract for safety from the very beginning.

Couple therapy can be provocative and stimulate an angry and potentially dangerous response following a session. In cases of potential physical abuse, I always insist that each member of the couple have individual treatment, an agreement that couple therapy will be suspended if there's any physical abuse or even the threat of it, and that an anger management program like Emerge be completed before couple treatment can be reinstated.

We don't start the actual couple therapy until we've fully evaluated and addressed the potential for physical abuse first. Since many couples come in to therapy minimizing physical abuse issues, it is incumbent on the therapist to raise the question through questions such as, "Has there ever been an incidence in which there has been physical abuse by either one of you?" and if the answer is positive to address the issue first.

I recently had a case in which a couple acknowledged physical abuse had occurred in their relationship in the past, but they thought they had dealt with it effectively in a prior therapy several years before coming in to see me. They seemed to me to be in pretty good shape, so I didn't prioritize safety first. Three sessions later, after they had started working on some difficult issues, there was an incidence of physical pushing and shoving that was clearly dangerous. I really felt badly that I hadn't been more thorough in my evaluation and more careful in setting up a safety contract. We did establish safety rules and continued the therapy. However, I did not respond strongly enough to that one incident and now six months later, they are separated and struggling. It is incredibly important for all of us couple therapist to always put safety first and not minimize even small regressions.

Mental Illness

Often, couples will present with one member having a significant mental illness problem like depression, anxiety, agoraphobia, manic depression, or suicidality. When mental illness issues are the presenting problem, I help the couple become a collaborative team around dealing with the symptoms. We work together around getting appropriate treatment for the individual, whether that is a hospitalization, medication, or an individual therapy.

The more difficult circumstances tend to be when one member of the couple is reporting that their partner has a serious emotional problem and the accused partner is retaliating by blaming their difficulties on the marriage and/or their spouse. As in all these cases that present a conflict over whether the marriage or the individual in the marriage is the issue, the therapist's job is to help the couples create their own plan about how best to discern and negotiate their priorities for treatment. However, it's often not so simple

When Jason and Marisa came in for treatment, it was apparent that Marisa was severely depressed. She was spending much of the day in bed, not attending well to their two school-age children, and even ruminating about whether everyone might be better off if she weren't around anymore. However, the couple was also in a crisis because they were facing Jason's work pressure: he was being forced to relocate his family to Phoenix or risk losing his job.

In the first interview, it seemed pretty obvious that Marisa's symptoms had flared up in direct response to the threat of Jason's job relocation. In her own way, she was conducting a sit-down strike. Instead of being supportive and worried, Jason accused her of sabotaging his career and berated her for being selfish. She seemed to be having a real mental health crisis while Jason was experiencing it as a relational form of passive-aggressive behavior.

After a while, she crumpled into tearful silence. It rapidly became apparent that we weren't easily going to have a collaborative conversation about treatment priorities. I felt Marisa was at real risk while Jason was perceiving her as being manipulative.

In these kinds of circumstances, it's easy for most of us to get overwhelmed. That was my first response to seeing and hearing them. My simple guideline that informs all of my work is "Safety first." Even though there seemed to be an element of truth to Jason's accusation and Marisa's blaming him for her depression, the possible threat of suicidality had to be dealt with first and foremost.

"Jason and Marisa, I don't know you well, but given what I am hearing, it seems like we have to consider getting you, Marisa, some immediate help. When a mom is feeling so desperate that she feels like everyone else might be better off without her, and 'everyone' includes your six-year-old daughter and your nine-year-old son, I am really worried. I would like to make a call right now."

Jason looked startled and shrugged. And, to my surprise, Marisa whispered, "Thank you."

It wasn't collaborative couple therapy; it was an emergency.

Throughout this book I have been offering case examples that reflect how I do my work built around empowering couples to take ownership of their own treatment plans in a collaborative process. Sounds good on paper. But sometimes the plans go out the window and the therapist has to react with gut feel and take charge. In the next chapter, we will talk more about our cases when nothing is going according to plan.

12

MAYHEM, MOVES, MISTAKES, MISMATCHES

The first interview with Fran and Greg got off to a rough start. From the moment they walked in, she relentlessly berated him about his affair with their underage teenage babysitter. He sat on the sofa looking sullen and frozen.

Although his behavior had been appalling, I wanted her to slow down her aggressive attacks so that I might find a way of connecting to him. I also didn't want my own intense, critical reaction to him to lead me to join Fran too much in ganging up on him.

So I tried to gently encourage her to pause. "Fran," I said, "I get how incredibly angry you are at Greg and that you need to get these feelings out. But I think it's important for us to hear from him and see what he has to say."

She looked annoyed with me, but said, "Whatever you say, Dr. Treadway."

I turned to Greg and said, "What I am hearing sounds pretty extreme, but I want you to be able to have a chance to respond. Somehow we have to make this office a safe place for both of you."

"Well, you should know, Doctor, that it was only one time. She wasn't a kid, but seventeen, and besides she started it. And—"

"Fuck you, Greg," said Fran as she leapt up and ran out of the room, slamming the door.

There was a pause and then an engine roar, and the next thing was a huge crash followed by loud squealing of tires. She had rammed into her husband's BMW with her Lexus.

I followed as he walked out to his car rather casually, and he said in passing, "Well, that should give you a clue about what I have to deal with."

I didn't know what to say. I was completely overwhelmed and in a state of shock.

Mayhem

S*** happens in therapy. I've had a guy throw a punch at me, a teenager throw a bucket of water on his parents in my office, an attempted suicide by a client following a session, emergency hospitalizations of clients, and threats of lawsuits against me. Even though these crises don't happen very often, we therapists know that our work can be dangerous for our clients but also for ourselves. Our work does take emotional courage. We're not the police chasing down an armed criminal or a firefighter entering a burning building, but we do dare to open our door and our hearts to strangers every day. And yes, somehow, usually by the seat of our pants and by asking for help, we learn how to manage crises. We discover how to respond to a wide variety of threatening, emotionally out-of-control behaviors, both in the therapy room and between sessions. We develop a repertoire of possible techniques and interventions that will help couples calm down and feel safe with their own feelings and each other's.

Working with Couples in an Escalating Conflict

Most couples who have difficulty controlling their emotional volatility reveal that tendency early. It is important to inculcate an expectation of respectful and careful communication in the first interview. These are some of the techniques I employ in mercurial situations.

1) People often come to therapy with the assumption that they will be encouraged to vent, saying their feelings exactly the way they feel them no matter how harsh, loud, or mean they may be. Teaching

couples to not interrupt each other, to not make character assassination attacks and to not yell in the therapy room is essential in the first interview when folks are usually trying to be on their best behavior.

2) It is also effective to give a highly agitated couple time to settle down by issuing their complaints and anger to me. I let them know that they each are on the clock for a five-minute segment and they get to plead their case, and that I will respond with empathy and compassion to both of them. That frequently helps them settle down enough to get to work.
3) Sometimes couples bring their fight into the therapy room and immediately get into it with each other. I will offer them ten minutes to fight it out. After they have a fight in which they talk over each other and attack each other, I invite them to consider whether their angry interaction is helpful. Rarely does a couple ever say, "Yes, fighting like this is helpful."
4) When couples are highly reactive to each other and tend to get into emotionally intense, out-of-control fights, it is essential in the early stage of therapy to teach them a technique created by my colleague Claudia Harris called Red Zone/Blue Zone for differentiating between aroused emotional states awareness and calm open states. Red Zone/Blue Zone is simply helping couples recognize their own escalating angry/shut down/submissive fight/flight/freeze responses (Red Zone) and learn how to calm themselves down and bring themselves back into the present using deep breaths, counting to ten, muscle tightening and relaxing exercises, and calming visualizations (Blue Zone).
5) In situations where one member of the couple can't calm themselves down, I might offer to meet with them in another room or send their partner to the waiting room. Separating a couple for a bit works well.

Moves

As I considered the various ways I try to manage escalating situations in the room, I realized that I have accumulated a number of tried-and-true methods for maneuvering through couple therapy sessions. I thought I would share some of my standard "moves" or tricks of the trade.

1) Reframing.

Clients often assume their partners are out to get them and are being intentionally mean and hurtful. It is essential to help couples understand and appreciate that almost always each partner is responding out of being hurt and feeling attacked. That their mean statements derive from their vulnerability and efforts to protect themselves. Reframing clients' behavior in this way happens in virtually every one of my sessions.

For example, I might say, "I know both of you blame the other one for starting these fights, but my sense is that each of you is actually fighting for your own safety, even survival, in these moments. I know it's hard to imagine, but regardless of what the content of the fight is, each of you feels hurt, attacked, blamed. Ironically, even in the midst of throwing stones at each other, deep down inside each of you is having the same feelings of being hurt and misunderstood."

2) Normalizing.

As that last sentence illustrates, couple therapists provide a certain amount of reassurance to couples about their struggles. It is often a huge relief to a couple to be told that their struggles are pretty normal in most relationships.

People think they are the only ones who aren't having sex very often, or who have huge fights, or who nitpick incessantly. Reassuring couples, as in, "Listen you guys, you're talking as if there was something wrong with you that after thirty-five years of marriage, you're not feeling 'in love.' It's important to remember that for the vast majority of folks, even in the most successful marriages the romantic intensity and passion of the first years fades. That's what people mean when they say 'the honeymoon is over.'"

In addition to normalizing what a couple experiences, I also share pretty freely the up and downs, trails and tribulations of my own marriage because clients often put us on pedestals and it's a relief for them to know that our relational lives can be difficult too. I address this much more deeply in the upcoming chapter on therapists' self-disclosure.

3) Indirect messaging.

There are always three people in the room, and one of the ways that I can reach the more shutdown or defended spouse is by talking about them compassionately and supportively with their partner. Here's an example: "I know, Abby, that you often feel attacked by John, but I think the core of what's going on is he is in a lot of pain. Frankly, I think his criticism and complaints are really his tears. Just as you talk about feeling lonely, I suspect he feels lonely, too."

Often the soft indirect approach, a main characteristic of Milton Erickson's hypnotherapy, is more effective in reaching John. If I said to him directly that he might feel lonely he might very well deny it.

4) Multiple choice sales pitch.

Obviously, creating collaborative couple therapy is framing interventions in the form of choices. But if I am focused on a couple really taking on some level of increased change, I will often present the choices one at a time, working from most dramatic and difficult to the easiest and most doable.

For example, if I am trying to get Joan to confront her drinking, which we've been talking about a lot with little progress, I may start with, "Joan, you know how worried Stan and your kids and I are about your drinking and your health. I really think you ought to consider going into detox and then maybe doing a month-long program."

And she's very likely to reject that and say she can do it on her own. My second pitch might be to try some outpatient groups and some AA meetings.

When she turns that down, also, I might say something like this: "Joan, clearly it's really hard for you to consider more aggressive treatment and that you really want to do this on your own. How about if we work on your creating your own plan for careful and safe drinking."

Folks like Joan who have already rejected a couple of ideas frequently grasp the last choice, even it's hard for them, so as not to appear completely resistant and stubborn. Joan had been reluctant to come up with a controlled drinking plan before, but now given the much tougher alternative options, she was suddenly open to the third.

5) Challenging the more cooperative and engaged client first.

Usually one member of the couple is more committed to therapy and is willing to work harder and take more ownership of their part of the problem than their partner. That person is usually the one who pushed for the therapy in the first place. And approximately 85 percent of the time in heterosexual couples, that person is the woman. Their partner almost always comes into treatment defensive and resistant and ready to feel ganged up on.

When I need to challenge the more reluctant partner in the therapy, it is effective to challenge the more responsive, cooperative client first. This isn't necessarily fair in the moment, but it is effective. I might push Sally to be less critical and then turn to Alan and confront his temper.

6) Interrupting sequences.

Often when couples are stuck going around in circles in the blame game or in a fight, it's useful to interrupt the sequence by changing their seats or having them turn their backs on each other while talking to each other, or writing out what they want to say and taking turns reading what each other wrote, or utilizing any of the communication techniques, or talking directly with me rather than each other, or getting up and walking around the room, or just sitting in silence listening to a bell or meditating for a few minutes. And I could go on.

7) Mirroring.

I often will ask permission of a member of the couple to mirror their behavior if they are being aggressive or angry. For example, Andy was yelling at his wife and repeatedly picking up a chair and slamming it on the floor to emphasize his point. I was shocked at first, and then I interrupted him and asked quietly if he would like to see how he was coming across to his wife. He said "Sure," and then I moved closer to him to be the same distance he had been from his wife and took the chair and yelled, "Andy, this is what you sound like and are acting like with your wife." And I pounded the chair as I said it. His face turned white. And he quickly whispered an apology.

All couple therapists need a repertoire of ways we interrupt couples from just repeating their old dance. We each have our ways of managing and interrupting patterns of couple interactions. It's the heart of our work in the room.

I once wrote an article titled, "Learning Their Dance: Changing Some Steps." We all need a lot of new steps we can offer folks. What are your moves?

Mistakes

They sat in my office and said nothing, two sisters, a brother, and a brother-in-law. Their silence was heavy and thick. They didn't look at each other or me. Their eyes shifted restlessly around the room. The week before their brother had died. He had killed himself.

One brother was barely functioning, having spent the past ten years in and out of psychiatric hospitals. The sister and her husband had a marriage that was slowly disintegrating. The other sister lived alone and tried to take care of her siblings and the two aging but actively alcoholic parents. I had been involved in treating all of them at one point or another. I had helped them believe that they needed to live their own lives and stop devoting themselves to trying to rescue the family members in trouble. I had taught them about co-dependency and enabling. They had all been making progress.

In the days before the brother he died, he had called each one of them and, through a drunken haze, asked them to come and help him. He had made these desperate phone calls for years and years. They had always come. They had dragged him off to many hospitals. But his recovery was always temporary. It wouldn't take him long to return to the coke and booze. This time each of the siblings had followed my "tough love" advice. They all refused his demands. They told him that they would support him only if he took the first step and put himself into treatment. He killed himself instead.

I know I made a mistake. I should have encouraged them to get him into the hospital safely. It was a medical emergency, and I treated it as a therapeutic problem.

Yes, I followed the conventional therapeutic wisdom of the time, and yet he might be alive today if we had just gotten him to the hospital. This happened in 1986. More than thirty years ago. It still haunts me. I still treat one of his brothers and one of his sisters all these years later. We have talked through our feelings of having made a mistake. We hold our guilt and grief together.

All of us, despite our best efforts, make mistakes and potentially even do harm. I hate making mistakes working with couples, and I make them all the time. Sometimes mistakes can be careless logistical errors as in screwing up the schedule, not returning an email or a phone call, not remembering to follow through on something promised, and even not remembering critical information. However, the most harmful mistakes are relational when we hurt someone's feelings. Clearly there are a myriad of ways that might happen: empathic failure when we don't fully appreciate our clients feelings; talking too much about ourselves; basing our clinical judgments on our own experiences, displaying our own counter-transference reactivity; difficulty balancing the level of being supporting versus being challenging; becoming defensive when criticized; repeating the same interventions over and over again with the same results.

Working well with our mistakes begins in the first interview. I always acknowledge to clients that I might make mistakes in my work with them and that I can do my best therapy when clients are willing to give me critical feedback.

Then, when I do make a mistake or clients give me negative feedback, there is a great clinical opportunity to model for couples how to be open to criticism responsively and with empathy.

Here's an example: "Gee, Rick, I really appreciate you being direct with me about feeling ganged up on by Sarah and me. I certainly get why my flip remark about testosterone poisoning seemed like piling on. I am really sorry."

Taking ownership of a mistake without being defensive or trying to justify is almost always instantaneously appreciated. In the beginning of my career, I would get devastated by criticism, and now I see it as an intimate gift from a client daring to be open critically with an authority figure.

My responding with empathy and ownership to criticism can truly be a healing moment for some clients.

When Couple Therapy Isn't Working

Sometimes, despite our best efforts, our therapy doesn't work for some of the couples we treat. It's not necessarily because we made mistakes. Nor is it necessarily due to the couple being unable to be treated well. It isn't necessarily my fault or their fault. Sometimes who we are and what we have to offer isn't the right match for the couple sitting in front of us.

Many therapists, myself included, have assumed we should be able to treat whoever walks into our office. This is a truly erroneous idea. I am just not the right guy for some people. Maybe another couple therapist will do well with them.

I joke with my students that, "Next year all us therapists in the country will sit down in front of a special New Year's Eve broadcast and we will bring three of our least successful case folders, and at the stroke of midnight, we'll pass our worst case to the therapist on our right. In others words, we'll play Old Maid with our most difficult cases. And some of you might do well with mine and I might do well with some of yours and so forth and so on."

In collaborative couple therapy, discerning whether the therapy is actually helpful or potentially not working is a shared question for the clients and the therapist to be asking themselves throughout their sessions.

Even if only one member of the therapist-client triumvirate feels like the therapy isn't working and not enough progress is being made, it's important to pause the therapy and consider together what needs to change. I offer the following options:

1) If just one member of the couple feels stuck, we first try to address it in couple therapy. If we can't renegotiate what we're doing successfully, I will often suggest that I meet alone with the dissatisfied person to see if I can't get to the bottom of what's difficult for them.
2) If the couple and I are concerned about our progress together, I usually suggest we get a consultation together and I'll ask a colleague to help assess our therapeutic system.
3) Sometimes, I'll give a couple a referral to consult with a colleague without including me. Some couples will be freer to discuss what's not working in our therapy if I'm not there.
4) Finally, I recognize that some couple therapy can be enabling. Couples might stay in therapy without making the changes they want or succeeding at their goals because it's safer and more comfortable to talk about change with one's therapist than to do the work of actually

changing. Some couples might reassure themselves that being in therapy is doing enough. I call this a Therapeutic Discharge.

The possibility that the therapy process itself is becoming enabling happens most frequently when addictions are involved. I believe deeply in going the "extra mile," and frequently the extra fifty miles working hard with couples. I am a 100 percent all-in therapist. I give my time and my heart fully. But sometimes I have to remind myself of the old line from the 60s, "If you're not part of the solution, you're part of the problem." Sometimes continuing therapy is part of the problem.

In those cases, I gently but firmly tell couples that I can't continue working with them because I believe our therapy is not only not helping but actually hurting them.

After two years of trying to help Mary stop drinking and Chuck stop retreating into his porn addiction, I told them last week, "Listen guys, I know you think that therapy is useful to you, but I have come to believe that somehow our work isn't helping you deal with really destructive behavior that you say you want to change." I am a big believer in the phrase, "First, do no harm." "I have to say that at this point, I think our work is oddly making it easier for you guys not to change. We're going around in circles. I think you should either see someone else, or we should see someone else together, or you need to take a break from therapy. I honestly think each of you should take some time to consider the poet Mary Oliver's fierce question, 'Tell me, what is it you plan to do with your one wild and precious life?'"

They left the therapy, and I don't know what happened.

Therapy is unpredictable and not in our control. Our best efforts often don't work, and sometimes we do harm. And sometimes, it's just a simple mismatch.

13

THE ELEPHANT IN THE THERAPIST'S CHAIR

Sam strutted into the session with his hands on his hips, followed by Ginger, who walked in looking like a scared rabbit and rubbing her hands together as she shuffled meekly in behind him.

Once seated, Sam jumped right in and said, "You're not going to believe this, Doctor. She's frigid."

Ginger responded by bursting into tears and covering her face with her hands.

It was a rough start. I quickly got into how they both felt about "her" problem. Sam was very frustrated with his wife's lack of interest in sex, and Ginger was very upset with what was wrong with her and what had happened to her libido.

So the session went on for a while before I even managed to ask how frequently they had sex.

Ginger began to cry again, and after reaching for tissues, she said with considerable embarrassment, "We only have sex every other day now."

Sam looked to me as if to say, "You see what I have to put up with."

Internally, I was shocked. It felt like an abusive situation. I had a powerful judgmental counter-transference response. I was immediately pulled into wanting to *rescue the damsel in distress from the demanding ogre who was also looking to me for man-to-man support.*

So what did I do? I spent the rest of the hour reassuring and nurturing her while trying to kindly educate him about learning more reasonable sexual expectations. At the end of the hour he stomped out of the room the same way he came in, and I never saw them again.

With Sam and Ginger, I broke the cardinal rule of couple therapy. Don't impose my values and views of normality on a couple, allowing my own counter-transference response to dictate how I related to clients.

Virtually all therapists have a wealth of biases and judgments about the folks we treat and what might make them a successful couple. We are all shaped by our gender and sexual orientation, our relational experience, and our family of origin dynamics. Our life experiences and ways we have adapted permeate the therapy room. And naturally we have a tendency to offer the solutions that work for us. The compromises or settling we do in our relationships often may be unconsciously presented to our clients, perhaps as a way of validating ourselves.

My immediate reactivity to both Sam and Ginger kept me from joining both of them where they were and led me down the path of trying to be the knight in shining armor rescuing the fair maiden. It is essential that we therapists closely examine our assumptions and biases about relationships and how they impact our work with clients.

In addition, clients project on to us their biases about who we are and how we might think. It is not uncommon for a male client to assume that he will be ganged up on by his wife and a female therapist. This, in turn, may lead him to come in defensively, which then causes the therapist to connect more easily to his wife, which may, in fact, confirm his fears. On the other hand, I am frequently chosen to be the therapist not based on my extensive experience, numerous publications, and seniority, but because I am a male. Wives often pick me because they assume I will be able to engage their husbands better. Not necessarily true.

Whether it results from our bias or theirs, sometimes we therapists are the elephant in the room.

Let's look at some of the impact that our own life experience has on couple therapy.

Gender and Sexual Orientation

Most of us therapists are exceptionally good at making an empathic connection to virtually all our clients; however, our experience of our gender has a powerful impact, often with whom we identify with in the room. As Margie said once in an all-female supervision group of mine, "I don't know how to deal with guys when they make a big deal out of cleaning up the kitchen once. I feel almost as annoyed as his wife." All the other therapists laughed knowingly.

And I also remember an all-male supervision group in which we acknowledged our frustration with and reactivity to how little women seemed to have empathy and understanding about men's pain and struggles with unfulfilled sexual needs.

Often we try to compensate for our internal biases by bending over backward to be supportive of the spouse who we are most put off by. I recognize that sometimes I don't adequately challenge some wives because I am so reactive to them.

Along with our gender, our sexual orientation and experience can also lead us to unconscious biases and judgments about folks with a different story. Whenever I am treating gay or lesbian couples, I start with an acknowledgment of inexperience and lack of understanding of the norms of their culture. I ask them to be willing to both educate me and confront me when my biases or stereotype assumptions show up in the room.

Race, Ethnicity, and Cultural Difference

Last spring, I met with Janis and Roger, a black couple. The first interview went very smoothly. I did note that they were careful to establish their credentials in the world and let me know how highly accomplished they were. And I was also very careful not to treat them differently than any white couple. The session seemed to go well, and yet the unspoken reality of them being black and me being white had gone completely unacknowledged. Talk about an elephant in the room.

I really liked these guys and wanted to make a deeper connection. We had had quite a bit of humor in the session so I decided to be bold and made a joke of sorts to get the race difference on the table. I said, "So Janis and Roger, just like I am checking you guys out in this first interview, I am sure you're checking me out too. How did I do therapizing while white?"

Their surprise and laughter broke the unacknowledged ice. Janis said with a big smile, "Well, you're not half bad as a white therapist. At least you didn't try to tell us that some of your best friends are black."

When working with folks from different races and ethnicities, I always try to find a way of acknowledging our difference and my potential lack of understanding of their norms and culture. I explicitly ask for feedback if I inadvertently step on someone's toes. I had one black client respond bluntly by saying, "We're used to having to educate white people. Just don't ask me to speak for all black people and we'll do fine."

Every couple is a separate culture unto themselves. That's obvious when we're talking about a different race or ethnicity, but even the couples with a very similar social class and educational background as yours are different. I am actually more prone to project my own experience on the couples that look like my wife and me. And I can be just as frequently off base in my assumptions as when I am with a Latino couple.

Family of Origin and Relational Experiences

Each of us bring to our therapy our own family backgrounds and relational histories. Many of us grew up in dysfunctional families, and some of us have our own trauma histories. The calling to become a therapist often comes from our own childhood role as a caretaker. Coming out of my own painful history of being the co-dependent peacemaker in my family or origin, I took to being a therapist like a duck to water. However, throughout my lengthy professional life I have sometimes tended to be an over-functioner who takes on too much responsibility for my clients because of my own needs to make the therapy work. Sometimes that fosters a dependency on me and gets in the way of them taking full responsibility for their own lives. I also grew up very conflict-avoidant. Naturally I am very good at calming clients down and helping clients manage conflict well; however, my own tendencies often get in the way of my being able to trust the therapeutic value of some conflict that my clients are caught in. Sometimes powerful conflict is the catalyst for change.

And, of course, we all have some relational experience, and almost all of us have had our own hearts broken. Somehow we've found our own path to get us through the night, and it isn't surprising that we have a built-in bias based on our experiences. If we have stayed in a long-term marriage with a lot of compromise and difficulty, we might be prone to advocate "sticking to it." On the other hand, if we have had a successful divorce, it may lead us unconsciously to tilt toward the positive possibilities of divorce. Particularly if the spouse reminds us of our first partner.

***

Obviously, we wear our history with the color of our skin, our clothes, our age, and how our offices are decorated. No matter how careful we are to project neutrality and equal compassion to the couples we treat, our biases show and our clients project onto us their assumptions and biases anyway.

The challenge for us therapists is to observe ourselves and how we are feeling and reacting right alongside of tracking our clients. In addition to being attuned to my clients, I need to be tuned into my own responses so I can recognize how I might be inadvertently bringing them into the room. Sometimes seeing my own negative reactivity to one member of the couple helps me appreciate what the other member of the couple might also feel about her/his spouse. However, my challenge is then to be sure I find my own empathic connection to my client.

For example, if I had a do-over all these years later with my sexually demanding and entitled client Sam, I would treat my own judgment and reactivity as a challenge to address in me rather than one to take out on him. Often when I have these feelings toward a client, I will ask them questions about childhood hurts, feelings, and needs. If I can experience someone like Sam as an insecure, lonely, needy boy whose sexual desire is the only pathway he knows for expressing all of his heart's yearnings, than my heart can soften and I can respond to the pain he is in rather than the off putting manner in which he expresses it.

Sometimes, I become so frustrated and reactive in the room with one or both clients that I can feel the edge coming into my voice. I have to really pause to settle myself down. I literally need to start taking some deep calming breaths. I have even been so annoyed with one or both members of a couple that I have had to excuse myself to go to the bathroom so as to calm down. With Sam and Ginger, I got stuck trying to rescue Ginger and "educate" Sam. No wonder they didn't come back.

However, sometimes my annoyance and reactivity might be useful to share with the clients as a constructive intervention. Once I have become aware that my reactivity is leaking into the room with my tone of voice, posture, choice of words (as it did with Sam and Ginger), I need to find a careful way of expressing the feelings so the clients might hear me.

If I did have another chance with Sam, I might say,

"You know, I am worried that I might be coming across in a critical, judgmental way here that's not helpful and that I might also be coming across as overly protective of you, Ginger. I am concerned that the expectations you both have about how frequent sex should be and the pressure that puts on both of you. But there's no right wrong/good bad here. Our job is to find out what will work for the two of you. And just because Ginger is expressing her pain with tears doesn't mean you don't have your own deep sadness and pain, Sam."

This change in perspective would move me from the superior, expert position of therapist to a human being with his own feelings and concerns about my responses. I would acknowledge the way I was coming across might not be helpful and was becoming part of the problem.

Clients routinely project onto me the power of a judge or parent; the arbiter of right and wrong, good and bad. It is often useful for clients to see me to recognize my limited and flawed humanity right alongside of theirs. I sometimes utilize self-disclosure as a way of connecting to clients and as a way of putting us on the same playing field. In the next chapter, we will explore the complexity and power of utilizing skillful self-disclosure in couples therapy.

14

THE THERAPEUTIC USE OF SELF-DISCLOSURE

Pete and Ellen were feeling like failures because they have not been able to follow through on their homework commitments. I tried reassuring them that this is typical for most couples, but I wasn't getting through. They were feeling like giving up on therapy. I decided to be open about my wife's and my own failings at taking good care of our relationship.

"Listen, guys, my wife and I have been married for fifty years, and we have utilized all this homework well . . . except when we haven't. We can go for long stretches of time not doing our homework despite our best intentions. And when we don't do our homework, our relationship suffers. And what's worse is that we know better, and we still have long lapses. Not only that, but I am the more resistant one. The same guy that is exhorting you to do the work sometimes doesn't practice what he preaches."

"So what do you do?" asked Ellen.

"We don't spend a lot of time beating up on ourselves anymore. We just start over and do the best we can."

Under normal circumstances, many of us, clients and therapists alike, collude in not recognizing a simple reality: we therapists, are simply flawed and limited human beings too, struggling to make do in our own lives. And all of us have had relational challenges and heartbreak. Our clients tend to put us on pedestals, and sometimes we ourselves have difficulty feeling good as couple therapists when we are struggling in our own relationships.

Being open about the challenges in my relationship or my own difficulties as a spouse, despite my skills as a therapist, can be empowering and normalizing for a couple. Careful use of self-disclosure can be an incredibly effective intervention.

Many of us are unsure about how much information about our own lives—our personal experiences, successes and mistakes, beliefs and values that clients wouldn't otherwise know—to share. And how and when do we share in a way that serves their needs, not ours? We know from many clinical studies that the main determinants of a successful therapy are not our theoretical approach, years of experience, or type of training. The most important variable is the relationship with the therapist. Within that relationship, how much does it help or hurt the client for the therapist to share about themselves?

The answer is: it depends on the client. That's what makes clinically effective use of self-disclosure an art, not a science. Each client is different.

One day early in my career, I was a rehab group leader, and I asked a tough ex-con who had been in the group for six months what the most important moment in treatment was for him. Mind you, it was the early 70s, we had met for three hours a day, four days a week, and I had thrown every encounter group/gestalt technique possible at the poor guy. I expected him to pick one of his many "cathartic breakthroughs." Without a moment's hesitation, he looked at me and said, "The most meaningful moment I've had was that night when you had to discharge Carl from the group and you cried."

That unintentional self-disclosure somehow allowed Jackson to know how much I cared, and it mattered to him. My tears turned out to be a gift to him.

However, there was also the time when I was treating an older woman and her husband in couple therapy, and she shared for the first time in her life the details of having been sexually abused by her father when she was a girl. The story was so heartbreaking that my eyes filled with tears. I thought it was an incredibly tender moment between her, her husband, and me. She never came back for another session. Later I found out from her husband that she had said she didn't want to deal with a guy who couldn't handle her trauma history. So much for the gift of my tears.

Each client is different.

***

My professional life began in a culture in which clinical use of self-disclosure was highly valued. My first clinical job was in an addictions rehab center, Eagleville Hospital, where half the therapy staff were un-credentialed recovering addicts and alcoholics and the rest of us were master's level counselors. I saw the powerful impact of therapists being able to say, "Been there, done that." I could see how inspiring a recovering therapist could be, and I also saw the extraordinary healing power of the twelve-step tradition programs in which a healing community is created by people helping each other as peers rather through the hierarchical medical model I was trained in.

When I became a family therapist and began to treat patients who were much older than me and when I had not become a parent yet myself, I could see how much easier it was to work with folks if, instead of operating from the one-up "expert" position, I simply acknowledged my lack of hands on experience and asked them to educate me about their parenting experience as we learned to work together.

Sharing our limitations, failings, and uncertainties can empower our clients to be less judgmental and self-critical about their own human frailties. We put ourselves on the same level rather than leaving them in the chronic one-down stance of the doctor-patient relationship. When we ask for our clients' input about the therapy and what might be most helpful, we are inviting them to collaborate in their own healing and to partner with us in the work, which also empowers them by valuing their perspective and expertise on their own lives.

Self-disclosure can be a healing gift. It can also be a boundary violating, insensitive, inappropriate self-indulgence. Clients don't need to hear about our lives just because we want to share our thoughts or feelings with them. Too much mutual sharing can cause the therapy to become more like a friendship, and that undermines one of the central tenets of therapy: the client is encouraged to focus entirely on their needs and issues without having to be emotionally careful or caregiving with the therapist.

Here's the model for thoughtful, client-centered therapist's self-disclosure that guides me when I consider explicitly sharing a part of myself for the sake of my client. It is always an experiment that has to be conducted very carefully.

1) Hypotheses

   First, I have to make some assessment about what's going on in a session: how open the clients are, if they are stuck in a rut, if they are defensive in relationship to me. I ask myself, what's happening right now, and is it working? For example, I was once a consultant working with an alcoholic and his wife and their therapist in a demonstration interview where he clearly felt on the spot. As the session progressed, I could see he was becoming more and more defensive and was feeling ganged up on. My hypothesis was that the whole set-up of being interviewed by me in front of his wife, therapist, and a live audience was really jamming his circuits and that I needed to do something to reconnect to him.
2) Goals

   It is essential to have a clear idea about what your client's goals are and what your goals are. This clarity allows you to assess whether a session is going well or badly. We have to adjust on the fly to realign to our goals or even change them. In the demonstration interview above, one of my goals was to help the couple and their therapist work collaboratively on the alcohol issue without it becoming more divisive or adversarial. They had told their therapist that they wanted to achieve that also.
3) Strategies

   After reviewing what's going on in the room at that moment and how it aligns to our goal, we have to choose an intervention. In this case, with the husband feeling ganged up on by the wife, their therapist, and me, the big-shot consultant, I could have chosen to challenge the wife more or even the couple's therapist. That might have re-engaged him, but I decided to do that later and chose to begin with self-disclosure.

I had learned earlier in the session that Paul, the alcoholic, had grown up with an alcoholic mother, as had I. So in response to Paul saying, "I'm no dummy. I don't need to be lectured," I leaned forward in my chair and said in a soft voice, "Yes, Paul, you don't need to be lectured. And I don't blame you for getting annoyed. After all, you grew up with a mother who had a serious alcohol problem, much more serious than yours. I grew up with an alcoholic mother too, and I can remember just how mad I could be about all the people who tried to help but couldn't do anything but say platitudes and give lectures. That used to really piss me off, too."

4) Outcome

When you choose to self-disclose, you have to watch like a hawk for the outcome of your sharing. Does the client respond well? Does your self-disclosure seem to intrude on the session? Does it help change the tone or feeling of the session in a positive way? Or do people glance at their watches or come back with, "Well, what I was saying . . ."

I waited for Paul's response to see what the outcome of my sharing would be. He looked at me for a moment and then said, "Well, I know what you mean. It does piss me off when she starts bossing . . ." Then he paused and matched my self-disclosure with some of his own, "Look, I came in here on the defensive, because after all it's me doing the drinking." And then he laughed, and we were back on track.

***

Therapeutic use of self-disclosure is always an experiment. If the client doesn't respond, don't take it personally. Just move on. Try something else. Sometimes I have to remind myself that the therapeutic relationship is about the clients' well-being, not my own. It's not their job to reassure me if I share something about myself and it doesn't seem to resonate with them.

Unavoidable Self-Disclosure

Throughout much of the past one-hundred years, extending as far back as Freud's psychoanalytical psychotherapy, there has been an ongoing debate about the use and misuse of self-disclosure in therapy. This discussion about how much of one's own experience, thoughts, and values are clinically appropriate to share masks a simple truth.

In many respects, self-disclosure is truly not a choice. It's always a matter of degrees of self-disclosure. We reveal ourselves the moment a client is referred to us: our gender, our degrees, frequently our age and ethnic background. In the very first phone call, we show our interpersonal style, state of calmness, sense of humor, and level of empathy. And when our clients are in our offices, we are even more exposed, as they note what we wear, our hair styles, our weight, and how we decorate our offices. In the first session, they are checking us out every bit as much as we are assessing them. So regardless of how much we choose to say or not say about ourselves, in our every word and action, consciously and unconsciously, we are self-disclosing.

In addition, we are often going through our own life issues that are frequently transparent to our clients, like illness, or pregnancy, death of a relative, and sometimes divorce; even the success or failures of our children can be public knowledge if we practice in a small community. In these circumstances, our lives are even more of an open book. The choice isn't whether to tell our clients, it's when and how much.

Many of us are unsure about how much information about our own lives—our personal experiences, successes and mistakes, beliefs and values that they wouldn't otherwise know—to share. And how and when do we share in a way that serves their needs, not ours?

When the Decision to Share Isn't an Option

"And how are you?" That's been my opening line for decades. Until I got cancer. Then it belonged to my clients. When I opened the door to the waiting room, they jumped to their feet, startled. As if they'd seen a ghost.

"Are you doing okay?" they would ask in hushed tones.

My shrunken body, hairless head, and gaunt face without eyebrows or lashes revealed more about my being ill than any self-disclosure I could offer. Hiding behind my boundaries as a therapist's was not an option. My clients saw the truth.

All of these issues about useful self-disclosure were amplified when I was so sick I couldn't hide it. When my clients looked at me with great concern, I responded openly and directly. I gave them as concise and optimistic report as I could.

Invariably, one or both members of the couple would be like Bret and Elliot.

Bret was a blond, perky, cheerleader type, now a soccer mom in her forties. Despite three kids, she was in great shape and looked very pretty with skillfully applied make-up. She was disappointed that Elliot didn't seem the slightest bit interested in a sexual life.

"Well, Dr. Treadway," she said, "it just doesn't seem right for us to launch into our difficulties around intimacy when you're dealing with something really enormous."

"Listen, guys, obviously my illness does put everyday problems in perspective. Hopefully, you can utilize that awareness to be more tender and appreciative toward each other. This time in my office should be the one place where you feel like you can truly open up about the pain you carry and the struggles you have."

"You've got to admit it's pretty hard to deal with our sexual difficulties given what you're going through," chimed in Elliot, ignoring my reassurances.

So the session, which had barely begun, felt stuck. I didn't have any choice about disclosing about my illness. But I did have choices about how to respond to their genuine care for me and the ways it was blocking them from being able to utilize their session. I could either persist in encouraging them to focus on their own issues or, perhaps, help them by choosing to self-disclose even more.

Which I did. I rolled my chair a little closer to Elliot and Bret. "I need to be clear about something. I love my clients. I love my work. I hate being sick. Frankly, having the opportunity to work with you guys on your intimacy issues is a great help to me. I would much rather focus on how to bring flirtation and play back into your relationship than sit around worrying about my situation. So let's get to work on you and we'll all forget about me. And actually, you'll be doing me a favor."

I smiled at them. They smiled back.

"Well, we are making some progress," started Bret hesitantly, and then she blushed.

It seemed to work. My more personal disclosure that I needed them for my own well-being appeared to help. But isn't that a contradiction with the earlier statement that therapy is supposed to allow the clients never to have to take care of the therapists? Yes. It is a contradiction, but first and foremost we are simply human beings. In this case, opening up about my need to be the therapist helped Bret and Elliot regain their comfort being the clients. It worked for them. It might not for the clients I see right after them.

***

Clearly, I am an advocate for careful and creative self-disclosure for the client's sake. The value of self-disclosure has also proven itself in my thirty-five years of training therapists. We therapists practice an art, but feel the weight of expectation that we should be scientific and objective. No wonder many of us feel sometimes as if we are frauds or hypocrites. We look to experts to teach us and make us wise. We go to workshops and read books so we can feel that we know what we are doing, so we can feel competent.

But where do the experts get answers? They find the answers through years of hard work, constant pondering, and their life experience. The same as we do. Many of my students have found it to be reassuring that despite my being a successful, well-known therapist, I still have anxiety and confusion about my work. I still need to get help to untangle my unresolved issues from my clients, and I still make mistakes that do harm. It's the nature of our calling. Therapists are frequently relieved to know that none of us are exempt from limitations no matter how much experience, training, and skill we might have.

What happens in therapy may be a mystery. But therapists aren't. We are people with a calling: people who risk opening our hearts to the suffering of others. We believe that being one caring person, in one session, even for one moment, can be the difference that makes a difference. Learning how and when to share a personal part of ourselves that joins us with our clients in our shared humanity is often that difference.

15

OUR CALLING

Years ago, I conducted a little research project to assess the correlations among the therapist's perception of the therapy, the client's perceptions, and the observations of a researcher. A trained family therapist interviewed many of my former clients and recorded their notions about what happened in the therapy. She also evaluated these clients and made her own independent assessment of how well they were doing. Then she interviewed me without telling me the families' experiences or her opinions and recorded my recollections of the cases.

It was much like celestial navigation. We were going to take the sights of three different stars (so to speak) and then find where they intersected and that would tell us where we are.

The results were startling. Here's a brief summary of some of the responses.

The mother in one family reported, "Dr. Treadway saved our lives. We would never have made it without him." The two adult children and the father nodded in solemn agreement. Yet my researcher observed that the daughter was still severely anorectic, the mother was morbidly obese and frantically trying to manage everyone, and the father had clearly been drinking. My recollection of the case was that the therapy ended with no progress because the family's insurance ran out . . . but apparently, I saved their lives.

Another family that I considered one of my stellar success stories reported that the therapy had been ineffectual, but their situation had dramatically improved during the same time period because they had started attending church regularly together.

The coup de grace was the interview with my former client, Susan. I had fond memories of my eighteen sessions with Sue, who came at the behest of her parents her first week of freshman year at Wellesley. I don't have daughters, and hadn't done any individual work with a young college woman, but I liked Sue immensely. I remember trying to be a wise, kindly, safe man, in loco parentis, who might help her navigate a way through the treacherous waters of her first year of college.

Sue was in law school when she said the following to my researcher: "Oh, I remember Dr. Treadwell. He was a shrink my parents made me see a couple of times during the first few weeks of college. I don't actually remember whether or not it was helpful. He was a nice enough man, though." Then she paused before saying, "Oh, wait, I do remember something. One night he walked me to my car because it was late and the parking lot light wasn't on. I remember he said something incredible that changed my life."

My researcher asked eagerly, "What did he say?"

Long pause.

"Gee, I don't remember."

And when my interviewer asked me, I didn't even remember the walk to the car.

Did that one therapeutic moment really change Sue's life? What role does therapy play in helping people change their lives, anyway? Did my work with Sue truly help her? Is it hubris to think that what we do makes any difference at all?

I want to share a clinical story that to me reflects the privilege and pain of our work with clients. Our calling.

***

All four of Chip and Ann's parents had died of alcoholism before Chip and Ann were twenty. They were just twenty-one when they got married, and Chip was managing being the guardian of his three younger siblings. Chip was a factory worker, and Ann was a secretary; they were busy just trying to make ends meet.

When they came to see me in 1984, they were miserable—newlyweds drowning in the responsibilities of making a living and trying to parent Chip's three younger siblings who were living with them in their tiny apartment.

In the first session, Ann complained about Chip's drinking and he complained about her nagging. They readily acknowledged that they were completely overwhelmed by their lives, exhausted, agitated, and hopeless. The session was going nowhere, and then out of the blue I asked them about their first date.

They started to chuckle.

"Well, I wouldn't exactly call it a date, Doc," Chip said with a sheepish smile.

"No kidding," chimed in Ann. "This lug I had never laid eyes on before and I were huddling under the bleacher of a high school football game because it was pouring rain. I was freezing my ass off because I was in this stupid cheerleader outfit, and this guy offers me his letter jacket. Being the big hero he is," she finished with an affectionate tease.

"And yeah, she wasn't complaining, either."

Now they were both laughing with each other.

"And the next thing I know he's trying to helpfully warm me up by hugging me and that actually felt good, and then all of a sudden he was trying to kiss me and I yanked my head back and he planted a big kiss on my chin. The guy had no moves."

"You married me, didn't you?" he retorted somewhat flirtatiously.

"Fuck you, clown," she teased back, blushing

"Now, you're talking," he said with a leer.

They left the first session holding hands. And I thought I had done great work.

But the story continued. I worked with them for years as Chip's alcoholism got slowly worse and worse and Ann got to be more and more the classic over-functioning, micro-managing spouse of an alcoholic. I tried everything I knew to do and became somewhat of an over-functioning, co-dependent therapist. I was still a pretty young therapist back then. In truth, I ended up sort of adopting them. I just hung in there. But nothing changed until Chip had a DUI and finally went into treatment and began AA.

I only saw them occasionally after that, but I was truly proud to be invited to join him and Ann at his tenth anniversary celebration at his home AA meeting. Again, I thought I had done great work.

But the story continued. They came back in when both of their girls were adolescents. Chip and Ann fought all the time about parenting issues, and we worked together for a while without making much headway. They dropped out after a while because Chip thought that Ann and I ganged up on him sometimes. Then all of a sudden Chip was drinking again, this time aggressively and meanly. Ann managed to drag him back in, but he was defiantly belligerent.

He said, to us both, "My parents drank themselves to death. Why should I be any different. I'm not coming back here."

Two weeks later, Chip had drunk a ton of booze and gone missing. Ann called me in desperation.

"I think he's going to kill himself," she cried into the phone.

I felt panicked, too. "Call the cops," I said.

"What is the point of that, Treadway?" she snapped angrily. "They won't do anything. I am going to go find him." And then she hung up the phone.

I sat in my office and felt completely helpless. I prayed despite being a lifelong atheist.

And find him Ann did. For some reason, she drove to an abandoned train station which she knew was on his regular jogging route. She got out of the car and walked around to the back of the building, and there he was lying in a pool of blood. He had slashed his wrists badly.

She got to him in the nick of time.

***

Last year, Chip and Ann came for a friendly reunion visit and to proudly show me pictures of their daughter's first child. Chip's been sober for nine years, and now he's retired. Ann's thinking of retiring, too. They are talking about taking some trips together.

"You know it's all your fault we stayed together," Ann teased me.

"Not hardly. You guys were stuck with each other after your first date under the bleachers."

"I can't believe you remember that, Doc," said Chip.

"Let's face it, you guys are unforgettable, even though I tried."

The three of us shared a laugh. It was a miracle. And I was so grateful to have been part of it.

***

Looking back on my work with Chip and Ann, I don't see a lot of brilliant interventions or strategies. Often, I felt helplessly and hopelessly stuck. Sometimes all I did was doggedly show up. And yet I know I made a difference in their lives.

For most of us, being a therapist is a calling. Long before graduate school, many of us found our sense of purpose and self-esteem in caring for others. This was the way many of us connected safely.

Being a therapist allows us to connect deeply and intimately with people without having to be equally exposed and vulnerable. It creates potentially a kind of ersatz intimacy, in which the therapist is fully emotionally present, but on his own terms and within the boundaries of the professional relationship. Personally, being a wise and loving clinician has been a lot easier for me that being a husband, father, or friend. For years my emotional needs were too often more easily met in the safety of my role as a therapist. Emphatically connecting and helping with my clients' pain allowed me to vicariously work on my own unresolved grief from the relative immunity of the therapist's chair. I too have often given my clients my best self while giving my family only leftovers.

All of us have a profound responsibility to make sure our work, our caring, our love is in the service of our clients and not ourselves. Our vulnerability allows us to deeply connect to our clients, but it can impair our judgment and potentially cause harm. It's essential that we fully and repeatedly explore and work on our own emotional issues throughout our professional lives.

It is also critically important that none of us practice without ongoing support and supervision. We do not practice a knowable science. We are practitioners of a mysterious art. There are so many ways to make mistakes, overlook something, and get stuck that we all need to be reviewing our cases with a peer group or supervisor to matter how experience we are.

There have been times in my career when, out of my own mix of hubris and embarrassment, I have not followed this sage advice. Pride has led me to make mistakes and harm some of my clients. We teach our clients to ask for help scaling the difficult mountains in their lives, yet sometimes we think we should be able to do the climb alone. That's not safe for us or our clients.

Part of being a healer is to have our own centering practice in which we connect our small, insignificant lives to a pattern of meaning in the universe in whatever way we understand it. This sense of perspective allows us to stay humble as we respond to our clients' suffering and risk having a powerful impact on their lives.

***

Role of Spirituality

Many of us struggle to reconcile our rational minds and our yearning for spiritual connection. Years ago, a friend of mine presented a lowest-common-denominator description of the Higher Power that bypasses tangled questions of God and gets to the heart of the matter. We were presenting to some young graduate students on the subject of spirituality and AA. My friend, a talented social worker and a longtime member of AA, has a tough, blunt speaking style that sometimes is belied by the twinkle in her eye.

She said to her audience, "When I was an active drunk, I was an atheist, and I didn't believe in any of this God crap! Now I've been sober for fifteen years and still don't believe in any of this God crap!"

The startled audience froze. She glared at them and went on.

"There's only one thing you need to know to have the healing presence of the Higher Power in your life."

She paused. You could have heard a pin drop.

"The only thing you need to know about the Higher Power is You're Not It!"

Time and again I've walked into my office about to see dangerous, suicidal, out-of-control clients and repeated to myself the mantra "Remember, David, you're not it." Then I ask for help just like I did for Chip and Ann. I don't know if God is on the other end of the line when I pray, but I do know that prayer is good for me. It puts me in right relationship to the universe. It puts me in touch with how little I am. It breaks through my grandiose self-importance and sense of responsibility. It's not all about me.

***

My job is to do my best. But our efforts don't ensure that the therapy will help or even that we won't do harm.

I have on my desk a Jew's harp. Elena, a client whom I'd treated after her husband had had an affair, gave it to me. She went through a tumultuous divorce and a profound grief response. We worked well together. She gave the present to me as a part of our ending. Nine months after our last session, she came in for what she referred to as a tune-up. She seemed to be in good shape. I was quite complimentary about the progress that she had made, and it felt like an affirming session. Two weeks later, Elena killed herself.

There must have been some clues, but I didn't see them.

I keep the Jew's harp in front of me so that I might never forget her and to stay fully alert to the people sitting in front of me. I will never know if there was something I might have said or done that could have made a difference with Elena. This is the risk we take every day.

I know this. Our challenge is to dare to love with our whole heart

And if we do,

Grace happens.

Sometimes!

EPILOGUE

A raised eyebrow, a slight tilt of the head, pursed lips, or a shoulder slump was the language of anger and tears in the New England Yankee/Waspy family that I grew up in. We were always smiling and looking good. We actually were featured in *Look* magazine as a model, happy American family for their 1949 Thanksgiving photo shoot. We were so well-mannered and seemingly cheerful, one would never have guessed what lay ahead for the six of us: my mom would commit suicide, my father and sister would explode into psychoses, one of my brothers would suffer lifelong addictions, and my younger brother would struggle with addictions, but is now blessedly in recovery. And, of course, one of us became a therapist.

***

It began the summer I was sixteen. I was living at home alone with my parents.

My mom was depressed, overmedicated, drinking, and in bed most of the time. My dad and I went out to dinner a lot. That's when I tried to became their couple therapist. I would listen over dinner to my dad talk about how worried he was about my mother, and I would just listen and try to say kind things.

My dad and I would try to cheer up my mother in the mornings, dancing in front of her bed singing old vaudeville songs while holding pretend canes. Sometimes she granted us a small smile.

I tried to help her directly once. I said to her, "You know, Mom, it must feel terrible to just stay in bed all—"

"Mind your own business, David," she snapped back at me.

I felt like she'd slapped me in the face. It took me decades to understand that she was trying to tell me that it wasn't good or healthy for me to be trying to take care of her and my dad. Not my job.

***

I had been sort of a Prince Hal type, the third son; an immature wild kid with lots of partying and girl chasing as my main calling. But after my mother killed herself and my father and my older sister went into the mental hospital, and my older brother retreated to Florida and his booze, suddenly I was the head of the family.

I would spend my weekends driving up from Philadelphia, where I was attending Penn, to see my dad at the McLean hospital in Boston, and then on the way back to Philly, I would visit my sister in New York City at Columbia Presbyterian Hospital, where she had been taken after trying suicide herself.

For the first time in my life, I felt really good about who I was and what I was doing. I felt like I mattered. I felt strong and grown up. And I felt surprised and guilty that I wasn't feeling any pain at all.

***

Kate and I fell in love shortly after my mom died. We had been attracted to each other for a year or so, but the moment we truly connected was when she told me her dad had died when she was fifteen years old. My heart went out to her.

I understood how she was feeling, and she felt that.

I reached across the table and took her hand. Her tears came and, much to my surprise, so did mine. We both had lost a parent. We clutched each other's hands as if we were holding on for dear life. Naturally Kate assumed that our bond was that we shared the same feelings of loss. But we didn't. When I held her in my arms while she wept, I was connecting to her and her loss of her dad. I never felt those kinds of feelings about my mom when she died or even when she lived. Sadly.

Despite being college kids, we got married. My ushers made side bets that we wouldn't last a year. And for a decade we did struggle, trying to bring ourselves and each other up. Clearly we loved each other, and we had the profound bond of connecting around her grief, but we were also immature and I was frozen emotionally. We went into couple therapy. We had a six-month therapeutic separation. If we actually had been emotionally healthier and less enmeshed, we might have gotten divorced, but we hung in there, and our marriage blossomed into a wonder-full loving life together.

A year ago we celebrated our fiftieth anniversary.

***

Of course, I became a therapist. I loved connecting to the pain of my clients and being there for them. And I loved the feeling of mattering and being important in their lives. And connecting to their pain helped me feel connected to my own. From the safety of the therapist chair, I could borrow their tears.

It took decades for me to do my own work on myself, own my own tears, and not need my clients for my grieving.

When I do workshops for therapists, I often ask any audience how many of them recognized their calling to become therapists coming from their own childhood experiences and trauma. Typically, 80 percent of the audience raises their hands.

Yes, we were the sisters and the brothers who everybody confided in. We protected the younger siblings. We comforted Mom after Dad walked out on her. We were the peacemakers. We were good. We had our hearts broken. We took care of others as a way of taking care of ourselves.

None of us have gone into this line of work to be famous or make money. It is a pathway to our own healing, and that is why we often do dare to go the extra mile, dare to love our clients.

Sometimes, our own emotional needs get in the way of doing good work. I know in my case, my codependency can morph from commitment and compassion into over-functioning and even enabling my clients. I have had to work hard to do my own healing.

But most of us do work really hard on our own recovery journey. We are not simply wounded healers. And as we slowly heal ourselves, we bring that light and love to those we are privileged to work with. This is "paying it forward."

***

It is the dead of winter. The sun is a pale small disk rising behind the stark black limbs of the bare trees. My book is done. I feel glad and sad. I know I could have said more and said it better. This won't be a book that works for everyone. In the end, it's simply the story of how I go about trying to help the folks who come to me. I hope it is helpful to you.

***

Dear Mom,

You've been dead for fifty-two years. It feels strange still wanting to talk with you. But I do.

I just finished a book about my life's work. I've spent all my years trying to help couples. I've been pretty good at it. I think you would be proud of me.

But that doesn't really matter. I just wish I could have helped you and Dad.

APPENDIX

Homework Handouts

Formal Talk/Listen Exercise

One person talks about whatever he/she wants to for fifteen minutes. Every minute or two, the listener reflects back as accurately as possible what the talker is saying without judgment, rebuttal, or any other editorial comment, not even a positive one. The listener contains their reactivity as best they can. The talker can correct the listener if they feel the listener is missing the main points.

There should be two scheduled sessions of only fifteen minutes per week with a minimum of twenty-four hours between sessions. There should be no comment on what the talker discussed except in the talk/listen format.

Please remember that this clunky communication exercise is simply designed to allow each member of a couple to discuss difficult and vulnerable feelings in a safe manner. It is neither a decision-making nor a problem-solving technique. Don't judge the value of the exercise on whether it makes you feel closer in the moment. Frequently, it won't.

Interactive Talk/Listens

One member of a couple talks for three minutes while the other actively listens, and then they switch with the understanding that the second member of the couple has the freedom to talk about whatever they want to talk about. They can respond to what their partner says or start on an entirely different topic. Communication is often a subtle form of power struggle in which there is a covert competition about whose agenda is running the conversation. By having each member of the couple free to use their time however they want, they create a sense of spaciousness and freedom in their conversation that is actually quite startling.

Couples usually agree that they will do three turns each. It is essential that once the eighteen minutes of back and forth is over that they don't continue the conversation for at least twenty-four hours.

The Time-Out Rule

In any heated conflictual situation that is becoming hurtful, volatile, or potentially out of control, one member of the couple may ask for a Time Out, which stops the conversation immediately. It is essential that the couple disengage and give each other a breather.

Within a minimum of twenty-four hours, the person who was given the Time Out thanks their partner and gives their partner in return five minutes to finish their interrupted thoughts while doing only active listening

At this point, the issues are dropped until the next eighteen-minute three-by-three. If the issues involve negotiating something that is time sensitive, than it's possible to call for an additional 3by3 to try to get to some resolution.

Please remember to take T.O. early before the emotions become too aroused.

Tender Loving Care

We all need to be nurtured and made to feel special from time to time in our relationships. Too often we are under appreciated and taken for granted. Gifting is a way for partners to make sure each week that they are each taking a little time to give to their partner some tender loving care.

Key ingredients:

1) Each partner comes up with his or her own very specific gift and negotiates a time when they can get it.
2) The gift is behavioral and time limited, like breakfast in bed, back rubs, a special chore, favor, or treat, etc.
3) The partner doesn't have to be "in the mood" to give or receive. Just practice.
4) The giver gives without expectations of gratitude and receiver doesn't have to make sure giver feels good.
5) Learn to do this practice for awhile before applying idea to sexual gifting and remember, "Road to Yes begins in the village of No."

The Decision-Making Protocol

1) Identify the issue to be decided (any issue from something small, like whether to stay in or go out tonight, or medium, like summer vacations and holidays, to large, such as having a third children, making a career change, or buying a house.) I usually encourage couples to practice on exceedingly small issues first.
2) Think through your own needs and desires on the issue separate from considering what your partner might want. I call it "thinking selfishly first." Usually one member of the couple begins with what seems to them like a reasonable compromise without articulating their own needs. This often backfires in the negotiations because one person has already begun with a compromise proposal and may not be able to be even more compromising.
3) Express your wishes in the Talk/Listen format, explaining what you want and why. The partner actively listens and then states what they originally wanted and why rather than responding or debating what was said by the person who went first.

tend to take precedence. That's when some of the normal difference in usual male and female sex drives begin to create tension around how much sex is good enough, and then the issue of how does sexuality get negotiated well is the huge challenge. People tend to become either routinized into schedules or into low-risk negotiations like this,

"You wanna? Later?"

"Are you kidding after the day I had?"

This kind of exchange is not the stuff of Hallmark cards, but it manages to help people not hurt each other's their feelings too much. In some ways it's easier to initiate a romantic encounter with a stranger in a bar than with your bedmate of thirty years. It's difficult to reject your partner's romantic advances in a positive, affirming way.

4) All roads don't lead to Rome.

Each individual has their own pathway to sexual arousal and intimate connection. The traditional divide was that most men seemed to think sex was the best pathway to intimacy while most women needed to feel intimate before becoming sexual. However, as gender clichés are breaking down, the variability of sexual desires and level of frequency are also evolving. It is much more common for women to be wanting more sex then men nowadays, which is particularly painful for both genders. It's always been difficult for the person wanting more frequency to ask and get frequent rejections and the person wanting less frequency to always be in the role of rejecter while feeling pressure to engage in order to be a good spouse. This is even more painful when it's not reflecting traditional gender rules. Being a woman pursuing a man for sex feels terrible because she takes it intensely personally that the man is not into her. A man who is withdrawing from sex can feel unmanly and inadequate and anxious.

5) Unfulfilling sexual experience.

The reality of sexual intensity and satisfaction waning with familiarity is well known. Premature ejaculation, difficulty achieving orgasm or erections, and lack of desire can lead to a cycle of disappointing encounters and a tendency to experience sex as a job rather than a joy.

6) Everyday couple tensions.

   Conflict and stress, kids and work add to the diminishment of time and opportunity for romantic feelings. It's difficult for a mom to feel sexually interested in her husband if he was an hour late picking up their three-year-old at daycare. Often couples try to have sex by shutting out the difficult issues of the day, retreating into their own erotic fantasy world where the bodies are new, hot, young, and exciting and the action is an adventure. This is a fine solution for creating arousal, but it often means couples aren't really connecting to each other relationally, so the experience doesn't necessarily feel very intimate or rewarding. Making love can end up feeling more like masturbation.

7) Masturbation and Porn.

   Since virtually any sexually arousing image can be turned on with the flick of a finger on one's computer or phone, accessing easy stimulation and relief is available all the time. More and more frequently men and women are turning to pornography along with reliable sex toys as a way of satisfying their sexual needs easily and efficiently rather than turning toward their partner with all the human complexities, negotiations, challenges that two-person sex entails.

***

Tips for the Art and Comedy, the Magic and Frustration of the search for Sexual Intimacy

Ways to Talk

I'll tell you mine; you tell me yours.

This technique encourages couples to share, either in or out of the office, their earliest experiences (both good and bad) of their own gender, family-of-origin attitudes around sexuality, puberty, their own earliest sexual feelings, romantic feelings, and adolescent experimentation with love and sex.

Loving Fingers/Hurt and Angry Feelings

This exercise is one I usually do in my office. Each member of the couple takes turns giving and then receiving a gentle neck massage with their eyes closed while simultaneously allowing themselves to experience their full range of feelings, including resistance, fear, hurt, and anger. This technique helps them accept that they may have ambivalent and even negative feelings while touching each other and being closer.

Bedtime Reading

Couples read books on sexuality and intimacy, which can provide a much greater sense of erotic possibilities and experiments. Couples may also choose to read or look at erotica or pornography together. This helps couples begin to share their own likes and dislikes in this intimate arena.

Start, Stop, Talk, Start Again

This exercise encourages couples to begin touching and kissing, pause and share their feelings, and then start again. It helps couples stay connected and open with each other while beginning to be sexual.

Grieving the Loss of the Garden of Eden

Virtually all couples have some difficulty transitioning from the "in love" stage of a relationship to the "in life" stage. Usually each member of the couple deals with those feelings alone. Through this exercise, couples learn to share openly their loss of romantic intensity and to grieve the loss of those "in love" feelings together, which can be very tender and intimate.

Love Letters

Couples write some of their favorite sexual or romantic memories of the relationship or write to each other about their own erotic fantasies. This helps couples rekindle some of their old sexual sparks or open more intimately to each other about their private erotic fantasies.

Swish

Using this neuro-linguistic programming (NLP) technique, couples learn to diffuse the buildup of aversive feelings that result from their relationship and/or childhood history by practicing replacing negative imagery with positive imagery.

Things to Do

Traffic Lights

Couples learn to schedule days in the week when they will not try to be sexual (red light), days when sex is a possibility (yellow light), and days when some kind of sex is a promise (green light). For many couples it is a great relief to have some nights in the week where there's no pressure or questions about sex.

Tender Loving Care

Couples learn to take turns giving and receiving agreed-upon sexual behavior (gifting). Many couples are held hostage by the tyranny of mutuality, believing it's best if both partners are aroused and have an orgasm. Learning to comfortably give and receive sexual favors takes an enormous amount of pressure off the couple.

The Seduction/Rejection Game

Clients learn how to make sexual advances and rejections in a light, playful and safe manner. One member of the couple is tasked with making flirtatious overtures while the other has to find a flirtatious and loving way of saying "no, thank you".

Swimming Lessons

Clients practice giving and receiving sensual and erotic massages as well as learning to give and receive constructive feedback. This is essentially the type of sensate focus work developed by Masters and Johnson, and is a significant part of sex therapy. I use the term "swimming lessons" to convey that these skill-building exercises are not necessarily that intimate or fun or erotic to start. Almost everyone remembers hating swimming class but wanting to be able to swim.

Little Sexy Encounters

Couples are encouraged to experiment with "making out" behavior in places that are not likely to create pressure to have sex, such as in elevators, cars, or kitchens, and timing a make-out session to last no longer than three minutes. Freeing the couple up from feeling like they have to get aroused and have orgasms also is a pressure reliever.

Masturbation

Couples are invited to experiment with their own masturbatory habits in private and to explore their emotions as they masturbate. Each member of the couple may discover that masturbation can become a greater expression of self-loving and potentially more fulfilling. It may also open up some more intimate feelings about themselves and their sexuality than they might share with each other.

The Art of Mediocrity

This exercise helps couples set lower and less fraught expectations for their sexual encounters in order to relieve their performance pressure. "Ho hum, good enough" sex is as important in a long-term relationship as profoundly connected, intimate sexuality.

The Amends and Forgiveness Protocol for both Partners

1) Each member of the couple has as much time as needed to discuss the ways in which they feel hurt, abandoned, betrayed, and disappointed in the relationship while the therapist and their partner bear compassionate wisdom. This may take one or more sessions per individual.
2) The listening partner is than taught how to write an Amends letter that involves directly taking responsibility for having done harm, describing how they hope to insure that they won't repeat the harm, and a willingness to negotiate some kind of amends action.
3) The Amends letter is read in the session and the person to whom it's being read is coached about to write a Forgiveness letter which involves accepting the amends and expressing acceptance of the

partner's effort to change, and understanding that the partner is a flawed and limited human being not having meant to do most of the harm they've done.

4) The partner who made the amends now goes through the same process described above: of having their own turn to speak their hurts, hear the amends, and try to forgive.

The Amends and Forgiveness Protocol after an Affair

1) The partner has as much time as needed to discuss the ways in which they have been impacted by the infidelity of the other. They can share their hurt, angry, devastated feelings while their partner listens as carefully and non-defensively as they can. They do not rebut or explain. Explanations are never excuses. The therapist helps the partner who had the outside relationship be compassionate and caring about the impact of their behavior. This may take one or more sessions.
2) The partner who was unfaithful is then taught how to write an Amends letter that involves directly taking responsibility for having done harm, describing how they hope to insure that they won't repeat the harm, and a willingness to negotiate some kind of amends action which involves concrete behavioral steps for an extended period of time. Some examples of an Amends action may be the partner agreeing never to see the person they had the outside relationship with again, or giving up drinking for a year, or getting rid of a boat in which a rendezvous happened.
3) The Amends letter is read in the session and the amends actions are agreed upon.
4) The challenge of learning how to forgive is then discussed and if the partner is ready to begin to work on forgiveness, he or she is coached about to how write a Forgiveness letter, which involves accepting the amends and expressing a willingness to try to forgive. Forgiveness can't be legislated; it has to be grown over time.

Camp Treadway

The heart of the weekend intensive is helping you be more comfortable with each other's discomforts and differences, to be able to share your feelings without shame or shoulds, and to hear the other's feelings without taking them too personally. The core goal is for you to learn how to have and share whatever feelings you have without getting caught in them. Just share them and move on to whatever the next activity is on the schedule. It's not about having a good feelings or shared feelings, it's about learning how to feel close and connected with whatever feelings you are having.

The retreat begins generally on a Thursday for a late afternoon session of two hours to plan the time together and set the therapeutic agenda, then there is a two-hour session on Friday at midday, and Saturday at noon is the ending session. Then there's a follow-up session once a week for the next three weeks. The follow up sessions are critical for success in translating the gains of the weekend into your regular life. Keeping the exercises going when you're home is essential.

Outside of the time with me, the retreat is divided into three blocks per day (morning, afternoon, and evening) You will take turns being the leader of blocks until the last morning, where you will decide together about block activities. Each block will have a least two structured exercises followed by a check in (to be practiced in our first meeting). And each block is ended with another check in. In addition to exercises there will be plenty of time for recreational events on your own. This isn't all work.

However, it is essential that you commit the whole time to focusing on yourselves and the relationship. Please arrange thorough coverage for work and children. Plan on staying in a hotel. And not using electronics except for urgent situations.

Exercise possibilities: Pick two exercises per block from this list, one for the beginning of the block and one for the end. The block leader is in charge of the rest of the block activities of the block except the follower has to be able to say no if an idea makes them too uncomfortable. Sample exercises:

a) Assigned Mary Oliver poetry readings
b) Trust walk (taking turns leading each partner around for ten minutes with their eyes closed)
c) Trust fall (falling backward into one's partners arms)
d) Face, or hand, or foot massage (three minutes each)

e) Thirty second hug
f) Metta phrases (for themselves)
   May we be safe and protected
   May we have ease of mind and comfort of heart
   May we see ourselves with love and compassion
   May we be at peace
g) Twenty minute hand-holding, silent walk
h) Fifteen minutes each of sharing favorite or painful childhood memories
i) Back massage (fifteen minutes)
j) Review ten key ingredients to making a successful relationship
k) Talk and Listen exercise (separated by at least an hour)
l) Tender Loving Care exercise
m) Decision making protocol
n) Five minute make-out
o) Loving fingers—hurt and angry feelings
p) Seduction/rejection role play
q) Timed interactive T/L
r) Sharing childhood pictures and stories.

Therapeutic Separation Protocol

1) In the family house or in separate homes.

   Although it often works best for couples to be completely separate for a while, sometimes when there are children or limited finances involved it's best for couples to stay in the same house together, but in separate bedrooms. The understanding is that they will not be trying to be a couple but will work together to be good co-parents and housemates while really stepping away from working on the relationship.

2) Length of time.

   It's hard to decide how long a separation should be. In my experience, three to six months usually works best. Less time tends to have less emotional impact and a longer time tends to increase the possibility of each member moving on with their lives and giving up their marriage as time passes. Usually we initially set a length of time with the agreement that we will reconvene to reconsider the options at a designated time.

3) Co-parenting and visitation with children.

Couples obviously need to prioritize protecting the kids and providing as much consistence and care as co-parents as they can. I will often have couples bring the kids into therapy to explain what they are doing and how it will work. Kids do best when the adults seem to be working together and are maintaining the kids' lives and routines as stably and as predictably as possible. It's also important when couples are going to be in separate living quarters that, when possible, the parents move back and forth rather than the kids. Kids do best staying in their own home.

4) Finances and legal advice.

It's essential that couples negotiate finances openly and fairly. I also encourage couples to get a legal consultation about the separation so as to make sure that whatever agreements they make during the separation cannot be used against them in a potential divorce.

5) What to tell children, family, and friends.

How couples share with others about their marriage and separation others often makes a bad situation worse. Well-meaning family and friends may take sides as a way of trying to be supportive. I encourage couples to come up with an agreed-upon message that puts a positive spin on the situation, like, "We've been working on our marriage and have decided to separate as a way of breaking some of our old, difficult patterns and giving us some time to create new ones. We're hopeful that this might give our marriage a fresh start."

Obviously, the situation may be more dire than that sounds, but the couple's marriage is a private enterprise, and I encourage couples not to be too open with others. The exception to this recommendation is that each member of the couple should be able to have one or two friends or family as true confidants, with whom they can share fully. Couples are encouraged to be clear with each other about who their confidants are.

6) Choosing between monogamy or open marriage.

It is critically important that couples collaboratively negotiate their guidelines around fidelity issues. Couples split between continuing with monogamy because the introduction of outside relationships feels like too much risk to them and doing some version of open marriage, which for some couples is a central element in really being free of the marital bonds. The key here is for couples to collaborate on a shared plan and then keep to it.

7) Continuation of couples therapy during separation.

   When my wife and I separated for six months forty-five years ago, we chose to stay in couple therapy as well as to have one-on-one sessions with our couple therapist. The ongoing connection was essential for us to have a safe way of staying connected, and I don't think our story would have worked out without it. Obviously, our success doesn't make it right for everyone, but most of the couples with whom I do therapeutic separations stay in at least some ongoing therapy with me.

8) Contact with each other, and with the kids.

   In most cases, I recommend that initially couples take as much of a break from each other as possible. If the separation is going to be powerful, couples really need to disengage well for a stretch. This approach is clearly influenced by the age of the kids. With young kids, couples do need to have ways of preserving the kids' sense of family while the parents are apart. Often couples choose to have a family night once a week, even though the parents are being as separate as possible.

   After a couple of months, if the couple is feeling ready to explore more contact, they may experiment with "date" nights or doing some of communications exercises and engagements that they may not have been very successful during earlier phases of treatment.

9) Trial reconciliation.

   Rather than thinking couples are ready for recommitment after a time apart, even if things have gone well I encourage couples to give reconciliation a try before recommitting. They need to experience substantial change and progress while living together before being sure that they should stay married. Making it okay for them to still have some doubts and ambivalence actually takes pressure off and gives them a better chance at success.

BIBLIOGRAPHY

Bloomgarden, A., & Mennuti, R. B. (Eds.). (2009). *Psychotherapist revealed: Therapists speak about self-disclosure in psychotherapy.* New York: Routledge.

Doherty, W. J. (2003). *Take back your marriage: Sticking together in a world that pulls us apart.* New York: Guilford.

Donovan, J. M. (Ed.). (1997). *Short-term object relations couples therapy: The five-step model.* New York: Guilford.

Dym, B., & Glenn, M. L. (1993). *Couples: Exploring and understanding cycles of intimate relationships.* New York: HarperCollins.

Gottman, J., & Gottman, J. S. (2007). *And baby makes three: The six-step plan for preserving marital intimacy and rekindling romance after baby arrives.* New York: Crown.

Gottman, J., Gottman, J. S., Abrams, D., & Abrams, R. C. (2016). *A man's guide to women: Scientifically proven secrets from the love lab about what women really want.* New York: Rodale.

Gottman, J., Gottman, J. S., Abrams, D., & Abrams, R. C. (2019). *Eight dates: Essential conversations for a lifetime of love.* New York: Workman.

Gottman, J., & Silver, N. (1999). *The seven principles for making marriage work: A practical guide from the country's foremost relationship expert*. New York: Crown.

Gottman, J., & Silver, N. (2012). *What makes love last? Build trust and avoid betrayal*. New York: Simon and Schuster.

Gottman, J. M. (1999). *The marriage clinic: A scientifically based marital therapy*. New York: Norton.

Gottman, J. M. (2011). *The science of trust: Emotional attunement for couples*. New York: Norton.

Gottman, J. M., & Declaire, J. (2001). *The relationship cure: A 5 step guide to strengthening your marriage, family, and friends*. New York: Crown.

Gottman, J. M., & Gottman, J. S. (2018). *The science of couples and family therapy: Behind the scenes at the "love lab"*. New York: Norton.

Gottman, J. M., Gottman, J. S., & Declair, J. (2006). *Ten lessons to transform your marriage: America's love lab experts share their strategies for strengthening your relationship*. New York: Crown.

Gottman, J. S. (Ed.). (2004). *The marriage clinic casebook*. New York: Norton.

Gottman, J. S., & Gottman, J. M. (2015). *Ten principles for doing effective couples therapy*. New York: Norton.

Gurman, A. S. (Ed.). (2010). *Clinical casebook of couple therapy*. New York: Guilford.

Hendrix, H. (1988). *Getting the love you want: A guide for couples*. New York: Henry Holt & Co.

Hendrix, H. (1992). *Keeping the love you find: A personal guide*. New York: Atria.

Hendrix, H., & Hunt, H. (1994). *Couple's companion: Meditations and exercises for getting the love you want*. New York: Pocket Books.

Hendrix, H., & Hunt, H. L. (1995). *The personal companion: Meditations and exercises for keeping the love you find*. New York: Atria.

Hendrix, H., & Hunt, H. L. (2003). *Getting the love you want workbook: The new couples' study guide*. New York: Atria.

Hendrix, H., & Hunt, H. L. (2004). *Receiving love: Transform your relationship by letting yourself be loved*. New York: Atria.

Hendrix, H., & Hunt, H. L. (2005). *Getting the love you want: A guide for couples, 20th anniversary edition*. New York: Henry Holt & Co.

Hendrix, H., & Hunt, H. L. (2006). *Receiving love workbook: A unique twelve-week course for couples and singles*. New York: Atria.

Hendrix, H., & Hunt, H. L. (2013). *Making marriage simple: 10 relationship-saving truths*. New York: Harmony Books.

Hendrix, H., & Hunt, H. L. (2017). *The space between: The point of connection*. Franklin, TN: Clovercroft.

Hendrix, H., & Hunt, H. L. (2018). *The happy couple's secret: How to build a lasting, satisfying relationship*. Amazon Digital Services.

Hendrix, H., & Hunt, H. L. (2019). *Getting the love you want: A guide for couples* (3rd ed.). New York: St. Martin's Griffin.

Johnson, S. (2008). *Hold me tight: Seven conversations for a lifetime of love*. New York: Little, Brown.

Johnson, S. (2011). *Hold me tight: Your guide to the most successful approach to building loving relationships*. New York: Piatkus.

Johnson, S. (2013). *Love sense: The revolutionary new science of romantic relationships*. New York: Little, Brown.

Johnson, S., & Sanderfer, K. (2016). *Created for Connection: The "hold me tight" guide for christian couples*. New York: Little, Brown.

Johnson, S. M. (2004). *The practice of emotionally focused couple therapy: Creating connection*. New York: Routledge.

Johnson, S. M. (2005a). *Emotionally focused couple therapy with trauma survivors: Strengthening attachment bonds*. New York: Guilford.

Johnson, S. M. (2005b). *Becoming an emotionally focused couple therapist: The Workbook*. New York: Routledge.

Johnson, S. M. (2019). *Attachment theory in practice. Emotionally focused therapy (EMT) for individuals, couples, and families*. New York: Guilford.

Johnson, S. M., & Whiffen, V. E. (2005). *Attachment processes in couple and family therapy*. New York: Guilford.

Kleinplatz, P. J. (Ed.). (2012) *New directions in sex therapy: Innovations and alternatives*. New York: Routledge.

Lieblum, S. R. (Ed.). (2010). *Treating sexual desire disorders: A clinical casebook*. New York: Guilford.

Nelson, T. (2012a). *Getting the sex you want: Shed your inhibitions and reach new heights of passion together*. Beverly, MA: Quiver.

Nelson, T. (2012b). *The new monogamy: Redefining your relationship after infidelity*. Oakland, CA: New Harbinger.

Nelson, T. (2019). *When you're the one who cheats*. Toronto: RL Publishing Corp.

Perel, E. (2006). *Mating in captivity: Reconciling the erotic and the domestic.* New York: HarperCollins.

Perel, E. (2007). *Mating in captivity: Unlocking erotic intelligence.* New York: Harper Paperback.

Perel, E. (2017). *The state of affairs: Rethinking infidelity.* New York: HarperCollins.

Real, T. (2002). *How can I get through to you? Closing the intimacy gap between men and women.* New York: Scribner.

Real, T. (2007). *The new rules of marriage: What you need to know to make love work.* New York: Ballantine.

Schnarch, D. (1991). *Constructing the sexual crucible: An integration of sexual and marital therapy.* New York: Norton.

Schnarch, D. (1997). *Passionate marriage: Keeping love and intimacy alive in committed relationships.* New York: Norton.

Schnarch, D. (2002). *Resurrecting sex: Solving sexual problems and revolutionizing your relationship.* New York: HarperCollins.

Schnarch, D. (2011). *Intimacy & desire: Awaken the passion in your relationship.* New York: Beaufort.

Schwartz, R. C. (1997). *Internal family systems therapy.* New York: Guilford.

Schwartz, R. C. (2008). *You are the one you've been waiting for: Bringing courageous love to intimate relationships.* Oak Park, IL: Center for Self Leadership.

Springs, J. A., & Spring, M. (1996). *After the affair: Healing the pain and rebuilding trust when a partner has been unfaithful.* New York: HarperCollins.

Springs, J. A., & Spring, M. (2004). *How can I forgive you? The courage to forgive, the freedom not to.* New York: HarperCollins.

Taibbi, R. (1996). *Doing family therapy: Craft and creativity in clinical practice.* New York: Guilford.

Taibbi, R. (2010). *Doing couple therapy: Craft and creativity in work with intimate partners.* New York: Guilford.

Taibbi, R. (2017). *Brief therapy with couples and families in crisis.* New York: Routledge.

Taibbi, R. (2018). *Process-focused therapy: A guide for creating effective clinical outcomes.* New York: Routledge.

Treadway, D. C. (1989). *Before it's too late: Working with substance abuse in the family.* New York: Norton.

Treadway, D. C. (1996). *Dead reckoning: A therapist confronts his own grief.* New York: Basic Books.

Treadway, D. C. (2004). *Intimacy, change, and other therapeutic mysteries: Stories of clinicians and clients.* New York: Guilford.

Treadway, D. C., Treadway, K., Treadway, M., & Treadway, S. (2010). *Home before dark: A family portrait of cancer and healing.* New York: Union Square Press.

Wachtel, E. F. (1999). *We love each other, but . . . Simple secrets to strengthen your relationship and make love last.* New York: St. Martin's Press.

Wachtel, E. F. (2017). *The heart of couple therapy: Knowing what to do and how to do it.* New York: Guilford.

Weiner Davis, M. (2002). *The divorce remedy: The proven 7-step program for improving your marriage.* New York: Simon & Schuster.

Weiner Davis, M. (2004). *The sex-starved marriage: Boosting your marriage libido: A couple's guide.* New York: Simon & Schuster.

Weiner Davis, M. (2008). *The sex-starved wife: What to do when he's lost desire.* New York: Simon & Schuster.

Weiner-Davis, M. (1993). *Divorce busting: A step-by-step approach to making your marriage loving again.* New York: Fireside.

Weiner-Davis, M. (1999). *Getting through to the man you love: The no-nonsense, no-nagging guide for women.* New York: St. Martin's Press.

Weiner-Davis, M. (2017). *Healing from infidelity: The Divorce Busting® guide to healing your marriage after an affair.* Woodstock, IL. Michele Weiner-Davis Training Corp.

Wile, D. B. (1981). *Couples therapy: A non-traditional approach.* Hoboken: NJ: Wiley & Sons.

Wile, D. B. (1995). *After the fight: Using your disagreements to build a stronger relationship.* New York: Guilford.

Wile, D. B. (2008). *After the honeymoon: How conflict can improve your relationship.* Hoboken, NJ: Wiley & Sons.

INDEX

For Product Safety Concerns and Information please contact our EU representative GPSR@taylorandfrancis.com
Taylor & Francis Verlag GmbH, Kaufingerstraße 24, 80331 München, Germany

www.ingramcontent.com/pod-product-compliance
Ingram Content Group UK Ltd.
Pitfield, Milton Keynes, MK11 3LW, UK
UKHW022313250926
475702UK00046B/758

* 9 7 8 0 4 1 5 7 8 7 7 4 1 *